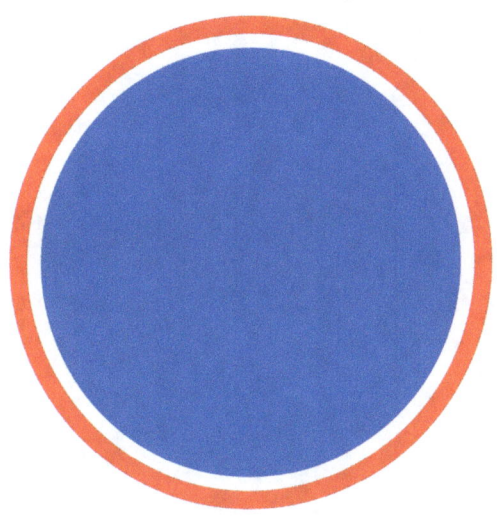

Speaking CTA

a conlang by Jack Bradley

Contents

I.   Introduction

The "CTA", or Chicago Transit Authority, is the entity which runs most mass transit in the city of Chicago.

It is a living antique. It is working, breathing, and moving. Sometimes bold. Sometimes lumbering. It is both relief and burden. Comfort and discomfort. It is a uniting force in a city that has relatively few opportunities to come together.

When I moved to Chicago, I was immediately enthralled by the monotony with which people discuss the CTA, the jargon that revolves around it, and the access that it gave individuals to the whole of the city. I quickly developed a desire to construct a language to give the users of the CTA as a clandestine means of expression, accessible only to those who pay attention enough to see it.

CTA's basic word order is subject-verb-object. There are seven parts of speech: noun, pronoun, verb, adjective, adverb, interjection, and conjunction. All roots in CTA are expressed by making a successful trip from a predetermined starting point to an end point. A word's part of speech is typically determined by the way in which the speaker's body is articulated. Because CTA is a ridden language and relies on a train to transport its riders from one place to another, it can easily take hours to say a relatively simple phrase.

Though the CTA itself is somewhat ubiquitous in Chicago, the language I've created for it remains and will remain, in all likelihood, clandestine. Still, who knows who may take up this dictionary and maybe thumb through it or give the phrase book at the back a quick look and give speaking CTA a whirl? Who in your commute this morning was truly participating in a hidden conversation? What are your fellow commuters saying through their own rides?

Love, sedition, praise, joy, friendship, envy, boredom, dismay, irritation, redemption, enthusiasm, unhappiness, gratitude, remorse, tension, analysis...What will you say?

II.   Notation

A standard notation system is used through this text in order to easily and fluidly describe the language.

Bite Lower Lip	*BLL*	Hand Near Face	*AH2F*
Blinking	*BNK*	Hand to Thigh	*H2T*
Clockwise	*CW*	Hug	*H*
Counter-Clockwise	*CntCW*	Left Eye Closed	*LEC*
Cross Legs	*CL*	Raise Eyebrows	*RE*
Eyes Closed	*EC*	Raise Heels	*RH*
Eyes Open	*EO*	Right Eye Closed	*REC*
Eyes to Left	*E2L*	Shake Hands	*SH*
Eyes to Right	*E2R*	Shake Head	*SYH*
Eyes Wide Open	*EWO*	Sit	*S*
Freestyle	*FS*	Tap Feet	*TF*
Grab	*G*	Tap Fist to Opposite Shoulder	*TFOS*
Grab Ear	*GE*	Tongue On Lower Lip	*TLL*
Hand to Chest	*H2C*	Transfer	*TNFR*
Hand to Face	*H2F*	Turnstile In	*TI*
Hand to Knee	*H2K*	Turnstile Out	*TO*
Hand to Lower Back	*H2LB*		

III.   The Stations

As stated in the introduction, the main medium for the CTA language is the elevated train system in the city of Chicago. Though perhaps expected by some, Metra stops and bus lines are not a part of the CTA language as described in this grammar.

The train stops are subdivided into two categories: **Loop Stations** and **non-Loop Stations**.

Non-Loop stations make up the bulk of the vocabulary and are utilized in most descriptor words.

Loop Stations, on the other hand, are utilized principally for creating clauses and posing questions.

Each train line is generally associated with a number of broad concepts listed here:

Green	east/west, left/right, movement/action
Red	north/south, up/down, studies/academia, sports
Blue	arts, clothing, body
Brown	structure, people, industry, place, number
Pink	serenity, peace, time
Orange	travel/transport, weight, size, weather
Yellow	thought, belief/religion
Purple	nature, money, math

What follows is a complete list of all "L" stops used in CTA vocabulary organized by line. Note that while some of the lines listed do extend into the Loop, the Loop stations are never used in descriptive words, with the exception of a few vocabulary words that pass through, but never stop in, the Loop.

Green Line	Red Line
◊ Harlem/Lake	◊ Red Howard
◊ Green Oak Park	◊ Jarvis
◊ Ridgeland	◊ Morse
◊ Green Austin	◊ Loyola
◊ Green Central	◊ Granville
◊ Laramie	◊ Thorndale
◊ Green Cicero	◊ Bryn Mawr
◊ Green Pulaski	◊ Berwyn
◊ Conservatory-Central Park Drive	◊ Argyle
◊ Green Kedzie	◊ Lawrence
◊ Green California	◊ Wilson
◊ Green Ashland	◊ Sheridan
◊ Morgan	◊ Red Addison
◊ Green Clinton	◊ Red Belmont
◊ Green Roosevelt	◊ Red Fullerton
◊ Cermak-McCormick Place	◊ North/Clybourn
◊ 35th-Bronzeville-IIT	◊ Clark/Division
◊ Indiana	◊ Red Chicago
◊ 43rd	◊ Red Grand
◊ Green47th	◊ Harrison
◊ 51st	◊ Red Roosevelt
◊ Green Garfield	◊ Cermak-Chinatown
◊ King Drive (goes away from terminus only)	◊ Sox-35th
◊ Cottage Grove	◊ Red 47th
◊ Halsted	◊ Red Garfield
◊ Ashland/63rd	◊ 63rd
	◊ 79th
	◊ 87th
	◊ 95th/Dan Ryan

Blue Line	Brown Line
◊ O'Hare	◊ Kimball
◊ Rosemont	◊ Brown Kedzie
◊ Cumberland	◊ Francisco
◊ Harlem1	◊ Rockwell
◊ Jefferson Park	◊ Brown Western
◊ Blue Montrose	◊ Brown Damen
◊ Blue Irving Park	◊ Brown Montrose
◊ Blue Addison	◊ Brown Addison
◊ Blue Belmont	◊ Paulina
◊ Logan Square	◊ Southport
◊ Blue California	◊ Brown Belmont
◊ Blue Western	◊ Brown Wellington
◊ Blue Damen	◊ Brown Diversey
◊ Division	◊ Brown Fullerton
◊ Blue Chicago	◊ Brown Armitage
◊ Blue Grand	◊ Brown Sedgwick
◊ LaSalle	◊ Brown Chicago
◊ Blue Clinton	◊ Merchandise Mart
◊ UIC-Halstead	
◊ Racine	
◊ Illinois Medical District	
◊ Western	
◊ Kedzie-Homan	
◊ Blue Pulaski	
◊ Blue Cicero	
◊ Blue Austin	
◊ Blue Oak Park	
◊ Harlem 2	
◊ Forest Park	

Pink Line	Orange Line
◊ 54th/Cermak	◊ Midway
◊ Pink Cicero	◊ Orange Pulaski
◊ Kostner	◊ Orange Kedzie
◊ Pink Pulaski	◊ Orange Western
◊ Central Park	◊ 35th/Archer
◊ Pink Kedzie	◊ Orange Ashland
◊ Pink California	◊ Halsted
◊ Pink Western	◊ Roosevelt
◊ Pink Damen	
◊ 18th	
◊ Polk	
◊ Pink Ashland	
◊ Pink Morgan	
◊ Pink Clinton	

Yellow Line	Purple Line
◊ Dempster-Skokie	◊ Linden
◊ Oakton-Skokie	◊ Purple Central
◊ Yellow Howard	◊ Noyes
	◊ Foster
	◊ Davis
	◊ Dempster
	◊ Main
	◊ South Boulevard
	◊ Purple Howard
	◊ Purple Wilson
	◊ Purple Belmont
	◊ Purple Wellington
	◊ Purple Diversey
	◊ Purple Fullerton
	◊ Purple Armitage
	◊ Purple Sedgwick
	◊ Purple Chicago

Loop Stations

Elevated:

Washington/Wells
Quincy
LaSalle/Van Buren
Harold Washington Library
Adams/Wabash
Washington/Wabash
State/Lake
Clark/Lake

Blue (subterranean):
Blue Clark/Lake
Washington
Blue Monroe
Blue Jackson

Red (subterranean):

Lake
Red Monroe
Red Jackson

The meaning of much of the CTA vocabulary is determined by the direction in which one travels. Loop vocabulary is no different and it is highly important to ensure that one is traveling **clockwise** (*CW*) or **counterclockwise** (*CntCW*) while riding on the elevated Loop tracks.

IV.   Use of Body

The use of the human body is the other main tool by which one speaks the CTA language.

These body movements sometimes require the sustained or momentary use of the entire body, such as entering and exiting a station or train. On the other hand, other movements require articulation of only a portion of the body, such as the hands, feet, mouth, legs, and eyes.

Use of the body serves a number of functions in CTA, including the marking of **case**, **aspect**, **mood**, and **part of speech**.

Multiple body movements may very well be employed at the same time, though physical limitations will ultimate curtail any simultaneous use of an excessive number of body parts.

V.   Nouns

A root is marked as a **noun** if the speaker grabs their ear while riding between root stops (*GE*).

When employed with nouns, the eyes determine the **case** of a noun. The **case** of the noun will determine its role in the sentence. CTA has eight nouns cases: **nominative**, **accusative**, **dative**, **locative**, **genitive**, **allative**, **ablative**, and **instrumental**.

EO

When the eyes are open, looking straight forward or in no particular direction for a long period of time, the noun is indicated as being in the **nominative**, the subject of a phrase.

Dempster-Skokie→   (belief)
Yellow Howard*EO*

EC

When the eyes of a speaker are closed for the duration or vast majority of a ride, the noun is interpreted as being in the **accusative**, the object of a sentence.

Dempster-Skokie→   (belief, as the object)
Yellow Howard*EC*

EWO

Eyes which are being forcefully held wide open indicate the **dative** case, which marks the noun as the indirect object of a sentence.

Brown Chicago→   (to the person)
Brown Diversey*EWO*

E2L

Eyes looking left indicate that the noun is in the **locative** case. This marks the noun as the location of something.

Merchandise Mart→   (at the market)
Brown Sedgwick*E2L*

E2R

If the speaker's eyes look right for an extended period of time, the noun is understood to be in the **genitive** case, the possessor of another noun. The possessed noun is always placed after the noun marked in the genitive.

Brown Chicago→   (The person's body)
Brown Diversey*E2R*
Blue Clinton→IC-Halsted*EO*.

LEC

When only the left eye is closed, this indicates that the noun in question is in the **allative** case, the place toward which something is in motion.

Merchandise Mart→   (to/toward a market)
Brown Sedgwick*LEC*

REC

If a speaker closes only their right eye, then the noun is in the **ablative** case, the place away from which something is in motion.

Merchandise Mart→   (from the market)
Brown Sedgwick*LEC*

BNK

Continuous and drawn-out blinking marks a noun as being in the **instrumental** case. The noun is therefore understood to be the mode by which an action is performed or achieved.

Irving Park→   (using the machine)
Paulina*BNK*

VI. Pronouns

The whole of the body is used to indicate the **pronoun** of a phrase. CTA has three pronouns: 1st person, 2nd person, and 3rd person, all of which may either be singular or plural.

Sitting down on a seat will express the 1st person (I/we) (*S*). Grabbing onto a handle expresses the 2nd person (you/y'all)(*G*). Finally, standing freestyle (also known as subway surfing) results in the indication of the 3rd person (he/she/it/they) (*FS*).

*G*Pink Ashland→Pink Clinton →Green Ashland	*you meet*
*S*Green Kedzie→Green Morgan →Green Ashland	*I hope*

One may choose to isolate a pronoun from a verb root for emphasis, clarity, or to utilize a noun case ending. To treat a pronoun as a lone entity, one must ride from one CTA stop to the next one over (direction does not matter) and exit the train. At the same time, one must place an open hand to the face, with the tips of their fingers typically touching the cheek (*H2F*) and the back of the hand facing up or toward the speaker's face. Proper eye movements are used to indicate grammatical case.

VII. Verbs

Verbs are expressed in CTA through tapping one's feet continuously while during one's ride (*TF*). Verbs have no tense in CTA, but may be inflected for mood and aspect.

EO

Eyes open, looking in no direction in particular, show that the verb is **indicative**.

$TF..G18^{th}$→Polk*EO*   (You do good)

EC

The **imperative** is indicated by the speaker keeping their eyes closed continuously.

$TF..18^{th}$→Polk*EC*   (Do good!)

The **imperative** may also be used to express a desire for something to happen, acting as the subjunctive. Thus, it makes sense to specify *who* you are ordering to do what. If your intent is to command a someone or something in 2nd person, it might be best to grab onto a handle (*G*). Though it may help with clarity, this is by no means a requirement.

24

EWO

The **negative imperative**, expressed in English as *don't*, is expressed by opening the eyes wide and keeping them that way for the duration or for the majority of a ride.

$TF18^{th}$→Polk*EWO*   (Don't do good!)

E2L

A verb is expressed as **imperfect** when the eyes are fixated to the left.

$TF..FS18^{th}$→Polk*E2L*   (He/she/it is/was/will be doing good)

E2R

The speaker indicates that a verb is **perfective** if their eyes look to and remain fixed to the right.

$TF..S18^{th}$→Polk*E2R*   (I had/have/will have done good)

LEC

Gnomic verbs (statements about general truths) are expressed by keeping the left eye closed.

*GE*Brown Chicago→   (People do good)
Brown Diversey *TF*18th→
Polk*LEC*

REC

A verb is understood to be **inceptive** (just beginning, starting out) if only the right eye remains continuously closed.

*TF..S*18th→Polk*REC*   (We start to do good)

BNK

A verb is **terminative** (coming to an end, or having come to an end) when the speaker blinks continuously.

*TF..FS*18th→Polk*BNK*   (They finished/stopped doing good)

The **passive voice** has two forms in CTA. The first refers to an action being performed by an individual or group who, for whatever reason, are unnamed or unknown by the speaker.

This is expressed by biting one's lower lip (*BLL*):

TF..FS Ashland→   (She is seen)
Green California→
Green Ashland→
Green California*EO..BLL*

The second form refers to a much broader passive voice where the unnamed participants make up an overwhelming large group. This is not to be confused with the **gnomic aspect**, since it does not refer to a greater truth, but rather an overwhelming tendency by large numbers of people.

This latter possibility is expressed by touching one's tongue to the upper lip (*TLL*).

*TF..FS*Yellow Howard→   (Everybody
Dempster-Skokie→   knows him/He is
Yellow Howard*EO..TLL*   known by every-
                              body

In order to refer to verbs in the **infinitive** or when **nominalizing** a conjoined pronoun-verb, one can hold their hand to their own face (*H2F*) while completing a verb's root ride:

*TF..FS*18th→Polk*BNK..H2F*   (The fact that they
have   done good.)

*TF..S*Green Kedzie→   (My going)
Green Clinton..*H2F*

*TF..*Green Kedzie→   (to go)
Green Clinton*H2F*

Negation is formed by shaking one's head continuously for the duration of a ride (*SYH*)

CTA's basic word order is typically subject-verb-object. However, this is flexible and a speaker-rider may place any of these elements at the end of a phrase to emphasis importance or relevance.

VIII. Adjectives

Adjectives are formed in CTA by tapping one's fist to the opposite shoulder (*TFOS*). CTA's adjectives always go in front of the noun that they are describing.

TFOS..Blue Western→
Blue Addison→
Logan Square...TNFR
Wilson→Lawrence→
Wilson*EO*

(cloth mammal, cloth animal, teddy bear, stuffed animal)

Multiple adjectives can also be stacked in front of a single noun or a noun phrase:

TFOS..Red Howard→
95ᵗʰ/Dan Ryan...TNFR
TFOS..Cermak-Chinatown→
95ᵗʰ/Dan Ryan...TNFR...
TFOS..Berwyn→Thorndale→
Red Grand...TNFR...TFOS..
Brown Belmont→Brown
Fullerton→Brown Wellington→
Brown Diversey...TNFR...
*GE*North/Clybourn→Red Belmont→
Red Fullerton*EO*

(Southern linguistic/cartographic station/nodal group, the South Loop)

IX.   Adverbs

A root is expressed as an **adverb** when a speaker raises their heels and keeps them raised for the duration of their ride (*RH*).

RH..Blue Grand→Logan Square   (aggressively)

Similar to adjectives, adverbs come before the verbs they modify. Though typically used to modify verbs, they may also be used to qualify other parts of speech such as adjectives.

RH..Pink Cicero→Pink Western...   (I happily begin

TNFR...*TF*..*S*Red Grand→   (to eat)
Red Damen*REC*

X.   Conjunctions

CTA has three **conjunctions**, which may be used to join or contrast multiple verb or noun phrases.

Each one of them requires that the speaker's legs be crossed (*CL*) while riding from one CTA stop to the next one over (direction does not matter) and exit the train.

CL..SAny1	and, so
CL..GAny1	but, however, though
CL..FSAny1	or

XI. Interjections

Just as with spoken languages, CTA also utilizes **interjections**. These are typically short, brief rides which often express spontaneous or strong emotions concisely.

An interjection may be formed in a formulaic manner, making use of root rides. When this is the case, an interjection is formed when the speaker undertakes a root ride while keeping one or both of their hands to their chest (*H2C*). This may be done in any pronominal position (*G, FS,* or *S*). No other grammatical maneuvers, such as noun case or verb aspect/mood, may be used with interjections.

H2C..Pink California→ Pink Morgan	(nice! lovely! how nice! how lovely! wonderful!)

Other times, however, the interjection is idiomatic.

Such is most often the case with salutations:

Hello: shake hands (*SH*)
Goodbye: speaker holds their palm open a few
                 inches from the interlocutor's cheek.
                 (*AH2F*).
I love you: hug (*H*)
Please: praying/begging hands (*PRAY*)

If an interlocutor is not present, the speaker may feel

free to mime these gestures.

XII. Questions

Questions may either have yes or no as responses. They may also require clarification on the part of the person responding.

When asking a yes/no question, the speaker raises their eyebrows and slightly tilts their head backward (*RE*).

*TF..G*Laramie→
Green Kedzie*EO..RE*

(Will you try? Did you try? Have you tried?)

*TF...FS*Irving Park→
Paulina*EO..RE*

(Does it work? Did it work? Has it worked?)

When asking non-polar questions, a speaker uses one of the following question words placed either at the very front or the very end of a phrase

Who/Which One	Washington Wells→Harold Washington LibraryCntCW
What	Washington→Blue Jackson
When	Clark/Lake→Adams/WabashCW
Where	Red Lake→Red Jackson
Why	Blue Jackson→Blue Monroe
How	LaSalle/Van Buren→QuincyCW
How Many	Clark/Lake→QuincyCW

*TF..FS*Red Damen→ Red Grand*EO*...TNFR... Washington Wells→ Harold Washington LibraryCntCW

(Who drinks? *lit.* he/she/it/they drink(s) who?)

Lake→Red Jackson... TNFR...*SAny1*..*H2F*

(Where am I? *lit.* where I/me?)

The response to these questions may be complicated. However, based on context, a speaker may be able to answer them with one or more of the following correlating words:

That person	Quincy→Adams/WabashCntCW
This one	Clark/Lake→Harold Washington LibraryCW
Then, this time (now)	State/Lake→Harold Washington LibraryCW
Here	Red Jackson→Lake
Because	Blue Monroe→Blue Jackson
This/that way	Harold Washington Library→ LaSalle/Van BurenCW
This many/that many	State Lake→Washington/WellsCW
Some	Adams/Wabash→State/Lake CntCW

XIII. Relative Clauses

Question words may also be used as **relative pronouns**.

*TF..S*Yellow Howard→ Dempster-Skokie→ Yellow Howard*EO*...TNFR ... Washington→Blue Jackson ...TNFR...*FSAny1..H2F*	(I know what it is. *lit.* I know what it)
*TF..G*Berwyn→Thorndale →Red Grand*EO..SYH* Clark/Lake→QuincyCW	(You didn't say how many)

The pronoun **Washington→Blue Jackson** (*that, that one*) is used to render the sentence succeeding it the object of the sentence preceding it:

*TF..G*Yellow Howard→ Dempster-Skokie→Yellow	(You know that I am a friend.)
Howard...TNFR...Washington →Blue Jackson...TNFR...*SAny1* ...*TNFR*...Central Park→Pink Damen*EO*	You know that I friend

XIV. Numbers

CTA has an octal numeral system (one based on eight). When specifying the number of a specific noun, the speaker places their hand to their thigh (*H2T*) instead of grabbing their ear (*GE*). They then tap their hand against their thigh for the number of times which corresponds to the quantity of the nouns they are discussing.

For example, if a speaker is talking about three toads, they might say:

H2T3SouthBoulevard→Dempster→South Boulevard

This system, however, will only work for numbers 1-7. For numbers 8-56, a speaker taps their knee instead (*H2K*):

H2K1:	*8*	*H2K5:*	*40*
H2K2:	*16*	*H2K6:*	*48*
H2K3:	*24*	*H2K7:*	*56*
H2K4:	*32*		

For 64-448, a speaker taps their lower back as audibly as possible (*H2LB*):

H2LB1:	*64*	*H2LB5:*	*320*
H2LB2:	*128*	*H2LB6:*	*384*
H2LB3:	*192*	*H2LB7:*	*448*
H2LB4:	*256*		

Numbers may also be combined together, with larger denominations coming before smaller ones:

H2LB6..H2K3..H2T6   *414*

H2LB1..H2K7   *120*

As is the case with pronouns, a speaker may choose to isolate a number from a noun root for emphasis, clarity, or to utilize a noun case ending. The process is identical in both cases.

To treat a number as a lone entity, one must ride from one CTA stop to the next one over (direction does not matter) and exit the train. At the same time, one must place an open hand to the face, with the tips of their fingers typically touching the cheek (*H2F*) and the back of the hand facing up or toward the speaker's face. Proper eye movements are used to indicate grammatical case.

XV. Non-CTA Words

Non-CTA words, such as proper names or foreign concepts with no ready translation in CTA, may be spelled letter-by-letter once just before boarding a train and again after disembarking at the next station, using American Sign Language finger spelling:

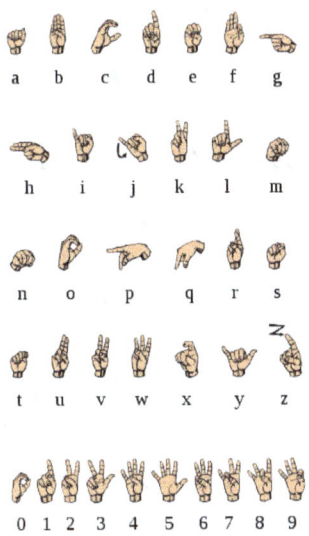

While riding from stop to stop, apply the appropriate gestures for part of speech, mood/aspect, case, number and so on. If a non-CTA word is a noun in English, French, Klingon, or whatever the case may be, it should also be a noun in CTA. Same for verbs. Same for adverbs. Et cetera.

Non-CTA words are capitalized in standard notation and their composing letters are separated by hyphens:

E.g. *Marie* → M-A-R-I-E

XVI. Topographical Writing System

While the notation system used in most of this book is a perfectly acceptable way of writing CTA, a student of the language may prefer to record their thoughts using the CTA's native writing system.

The word in CTA for *writing system* and *map* are actually one in the same. This is because written CTA takes into account the geographical position of Chicago's "L" stations.

Documents are therefore not written out left to right or in any particular direction at all. The place of a written ride on paper or a screen is influenced by its actual geographical location as seen from a bird's eye view. Up is north, down is south, left is west, and right is east. The order of the rides in a phrase is marked by an Arab numeral placed beside its corresponding ride.

Stations are marked by a circle with a colored ring, like this one:

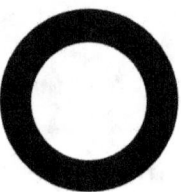

A three-letter call sign is assigned to each station. This call sign is written within the ring.

The color of a ring indicates the color of the line on which the station is found. If the color is black with no call sign (such as in the example given) indicates that the choice of station does not matter. Loop stations have call signs, but their rings never show the color of their corresponding line.

Two or more stations are linked by arrows indicating the direction of travel:

$$\circ\!\!-\!\!\longrightarrow$$

Below is a list of call signs organized by line:

Green Line

HAL	Harlem/Lake
OAK	Green Oak Park
RID	Ridgeland
AUS	Green Austin
CEN	Central
LAR	Laramie
CIC	Green Cicero
PSK	Green Pulaski
CCP	Conservatory-Central Park Drive
KED	Green Kedzie
CAL	Green California
ASH	Green Ashland
MOR	Morgan
CLI	Green Clinton
ROS	Green Roosevelt
MCP	Cermak-McCormick Place
BRO	35th-Bronzeville-IIT
IND	Indiana
FTD	43rd
FSV	Green 47th
FFS	51st
GAR	Green Garfield

KIN	King Drive (goes away from terminus only)
CGR	Cottage Grove
HST	Halsted
AST	Ashland/63rd

Red Line

HOW	Red Howard
JAR	Jarvis
MOR	Morse
LOY	Loyola
GRN	Granville
THO	Thorndale
MAW	Bryn Mawr
BWY	Berwyn
AGY	Argyle
LAW	Lawrence
WIL	Wilson
SHE	Sheridan
ADD	Red Addison
BEL	Red Belmont
FUL	Red Fullerton
CLY	North/Clybourn
CLA	Clark/Division
CHI	Red Chicago
GRA	Red Grand
HAR	Harrison

ROO	Red Roosevelt
CER	Cermak-Chinatown
SOX	Sox-35th
FSV	Red 47th
GAR	Red Garfield
SXT	63rd
SVN	79th
ESV	87th
DRY	95th/Dan Ryan

Blue Line

ORD	O'Hare
ROS	Rosemont
CMB	Cumberland
HRO	Harlem1
JEF	Jefferson Park
MON	Blue Montrose
IRV	Blue Irving Park
ADD	Blue Addison
BEL	Blue Belmont
LOS	Logan Square
CAL	Blue California
WES	Blue Western
DAM	Blue Damen
DIV	Division
CHI	Blue Chicago
GRA	Blue Grand
LSA	LaSalle
CLI	Blue Clinton

UIC	UIC-Halstead
RAC	Racine
IMD	Illinois Medical District
WES	Western
KHO	Kedzie-Homan
PSK	Blue Pulaski
CIC	Blue Cicero
AUS	Blue Austin
OAK	Blue Oak Park
HRT	Harlem 2
FOR	Forest Park

Brown Line

KIM	Kimball
KED	Brown Kedzie
FRA	Francisco
ROC	Rockwell
WES	Brown Western
DAM	Brown Damen
MON	Brown Montrose
ADD	Brown Addison
PAU	Paulina
SOU	Southport
BEL	Brown Belmont
WEL	Brown Wellington
DVR	Brown Diversey
FUL	Brown Fullerton
ARM	Brown Armitage

SED	Brown Sedgwick
CHI	Brown Chicago
MDM	Merchandise Mart

Pink Line

FCE	54th/Cermak
CIC	Pink Cicero
KOS	Kostner
PSK	Pink Pulaski
CNP	Central Park
KED	Pink Kedzie
CAL	Pink California
WES	Pink Western
DAM	Pink Damen
ETN	18th
PLK	Polk
ASH	Pink Ashland
MOR	Pink Morgan
CLI	Pink Clinton

Orange Line

MDW	Midway
PSK	Orange Pulaski
KED	Orange Kedzie
WES	Orange Western
ARC	35th/Archer
ASH	Orange Ashland
HAL	Halsted
ROO	Roosevelt

Yellow Line

DSK	Dempster-Skokie
OSK	Oakton-Skokie
HOW	Yellow Howard

Purple Line

LIN	Linden
CEN	Central
NOY	Noyes
FOS	Foster
DAV	Davis
DEM	Dempster
MAI	Main
BVD	South Boulevard
HOW	Purple Howard
WIL	Purple Wilson
BEL	Purple Belmont
WEL	Purple Wellington
DVR	Purple Diversey
FUL	Purple Fullerton
ARM	Purple Armitage
SED	Purple Sedgwick
CHI	Purple Chicago

Loop Stations

WAW	Washington/Wells
QUI	Quincy
VAN	LaSalle/Van Buren
HWL	Harold Washington Library
ADA	Adams/Wabash
	Washington/Wabash
STL	State/Lake
CLA	Clark/Lake
WAS	Washington
MRE	Blue Monroe
JAC	Blue Jackson
LAK	Lake
MRE	Red Monroe
JAC	Red Jackson

The following glyphs represent the gestures outlined in previous sections of this book. In writing, they are typically placed directly adjacent to the arrows of their relevant rides:

Glyph	Notation	Gestures
ᵁᴪ	*AH2F*	Hand almost to
⬭	*BLL*	Bite Lower Lip
⬤⬤	*BNK*	Blinking
⤳	*CL*	Cross Legs

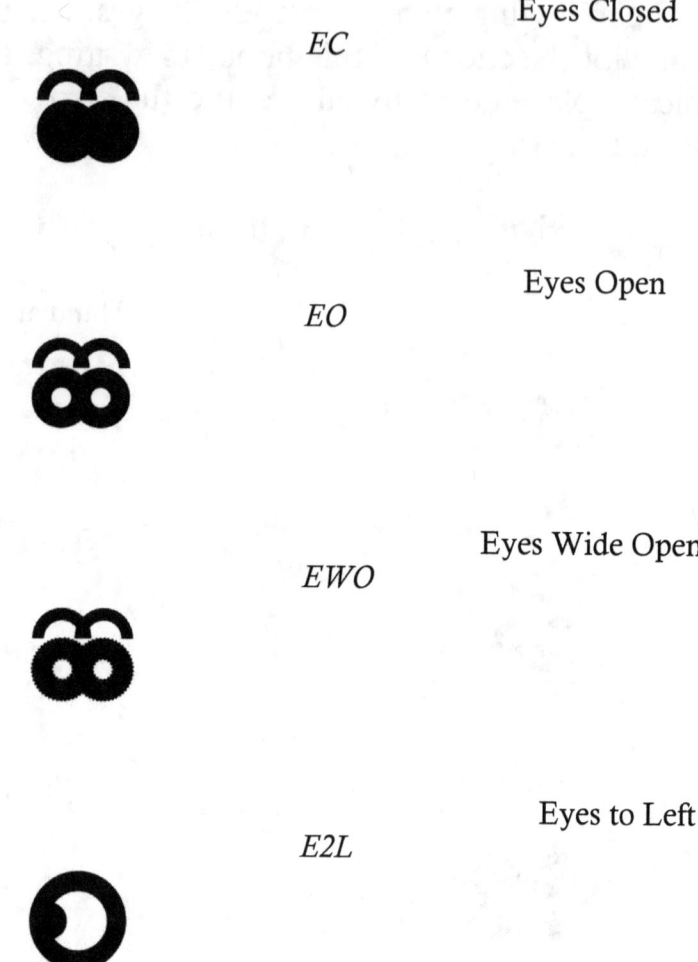

Eyes Closed

EC

Eyes Open

EO

Eyes Wide Open

EWO

Eyes to Left

E2L

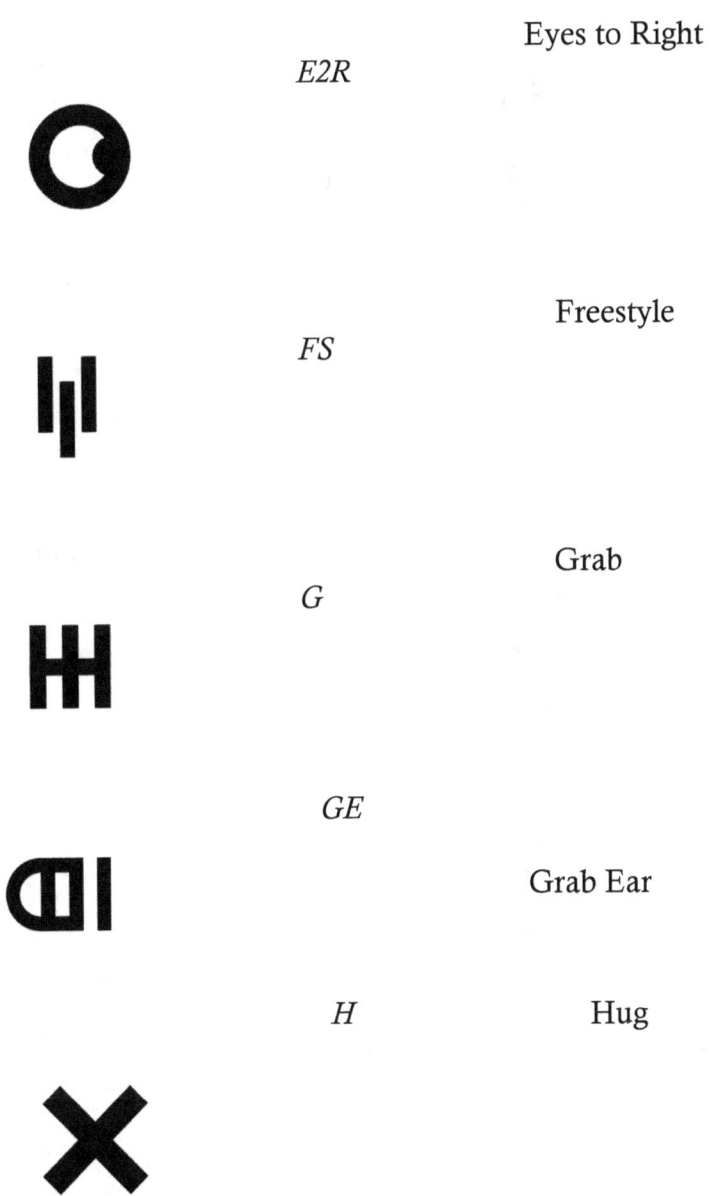

E2R   Eyes to Right

FS   Freestyle

G   Grab

GE

Grab Ear

H   Hug

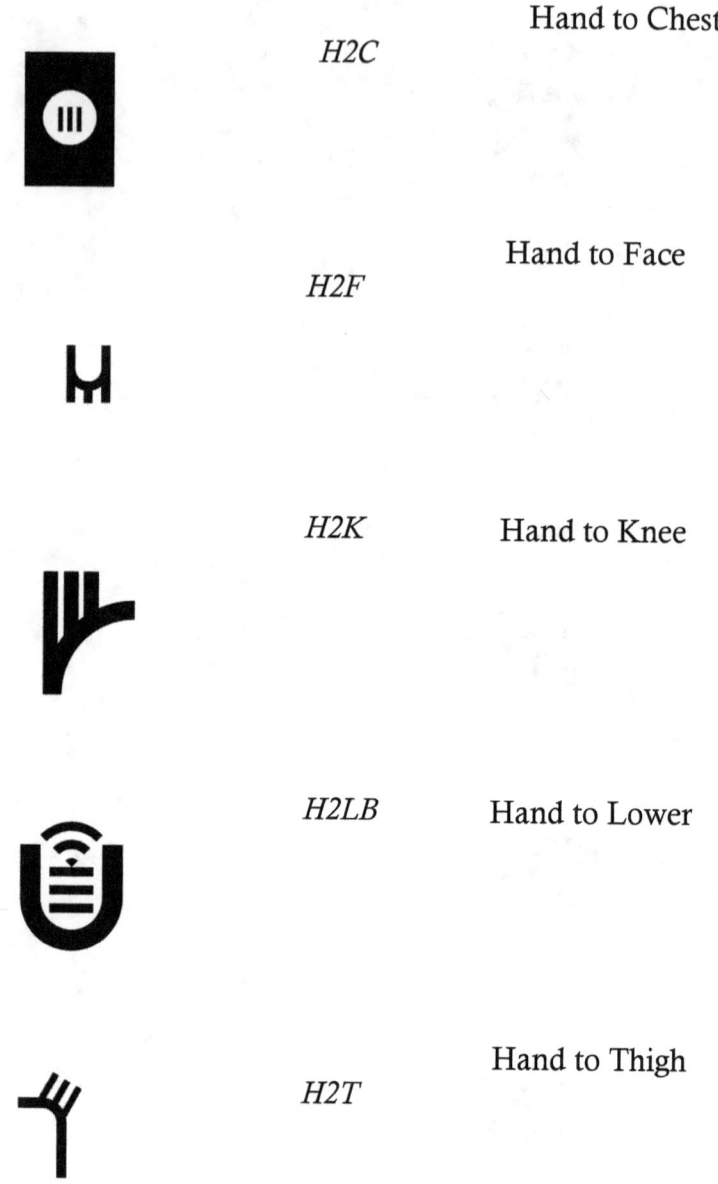

H2C	Hand to Chest
H2F	Hand to Face
H2K	Hand to Knee
H2LB	Hand to Lower
H2T	Hand to Thigh

LEC

Left Eye
Closed

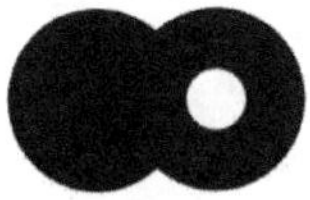

PRAY

Prayer Hands

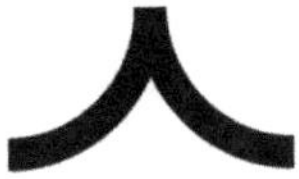

RE

Raise
Eyebrows

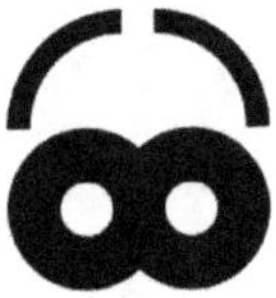

Right Eye
Closed

REC

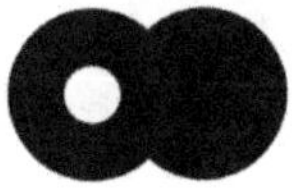

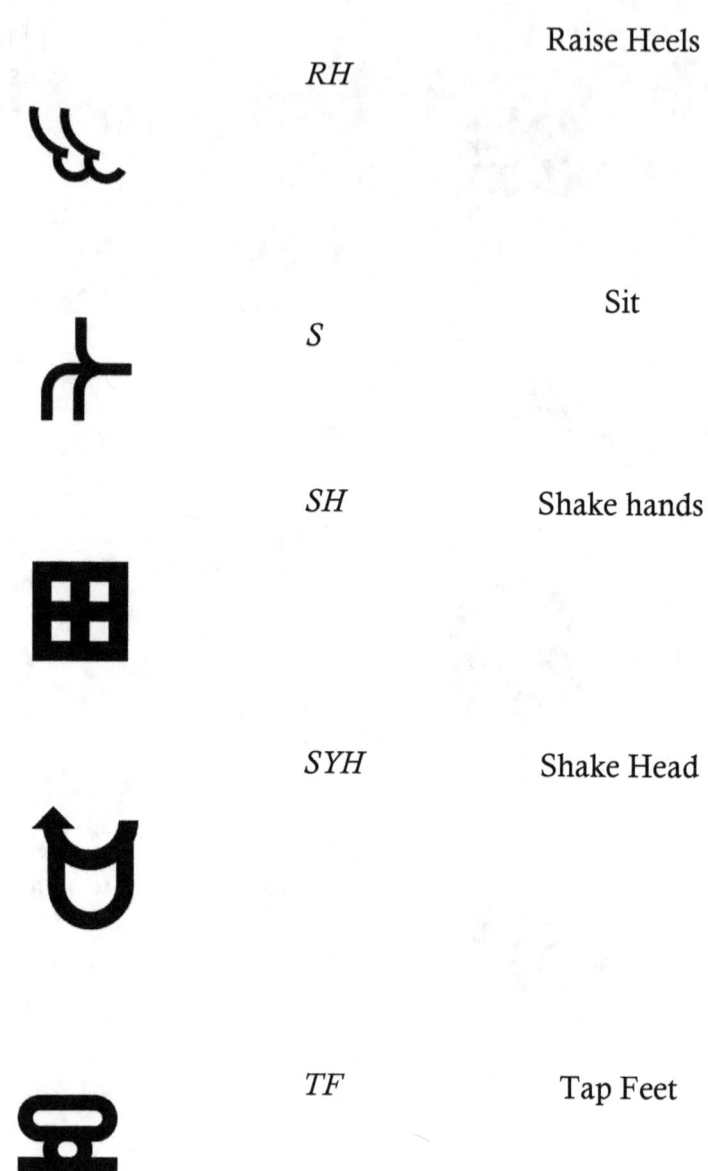

	RH	Raise Heels
	S	Sit
	SH	Shake hands
	SYH	Shake Head
	TF	Tap Feet

TFOS   Tap Fist to
Opposite Shoulder

TLL   Tongue On
Lower Lip

59

Dictionary

ability	noun	Cermak-Chinatown>Red Garfield
able	adj.	Cermak-Chinatown>Red Garfield
above, overhead	noun	North/Clybourn>Red Addison
act, action	noun	Green Clinton>Green Morgan>Green Ashland>Green Clinton
active	adj.	Green Clinton>Green Morgan>Green Ashland>Green Clinton
actively	adv.	Green Clinton>Green Morgan>Green Ashland>Green Clinton
aim (for), intend, mean	verb	Racine>Blue Clinton>Racine
air, freshness	noun	Central>Noyes
alcohol, alcoholic drink	noun	Green California>Green Ashland

alcoholic	adj.	Green California>Green Ashland
all	noun	Red Chicago>North Clybourn South
amphibian	adj.	Boulevard>Dempster>South Boulevard
arm, branch	noun	Noyes>Davis
art	noun	Blue Chicago>Blue Western
artistic	adj.	Blue Chicago>Blue Western
bean	noun	Clark/Division>Red Grand>Clark/Division>Red Grand
beautiful, pretty	adj.	Central Park>Polk
beauty, prettiness	noun	Central Park>Polk
beget, parent, father, mother	verb	Illinois Medical District>Blue Damen
behind, back, rear	noun	Brown Addison>Brown Belmont>Red Addison

belief	noun	Dempster-Skokie>Yellow Howard
believe	verb	Dempster-Skokie>Yellow Howard
below, beneath	noun	Red Addison>North/Clybourn
bend	verb	Orange Western>35th/Archer
between	noun	Indiana>Orange Ashland
big, large	adj.	Cermak-Chinatown>95th/Dan Ryan
bodily, corporeal	adj.	Blue Clinton>UIC-Halsted
body	noun	Blue Clinton>UIC-Halsted
brew, ferment	verb	Green California>Green Ashland
build, construct	verb	Brown Chicago>Brown Kedzie
building, structure, statue	noun	Brown Chicago>Brown Kedzie
bumpy	adj.	Red Grand>Thorndale
bury	verb	Red Grand>Red Chicago>Red Grand>Red Chicago

business	noun	Purple Chicago>Purple Wellington
business, business-related	adj.	Purple Chicago>Purple Wellington
buy	verb	Purple Belmont>Purple Diversey
call dibs	verb	Purple Diversey>Purple Howard>Purple Chicago
can	verb	Cermak-Chinatown>Red Garfield
captured, tamed	adj.	Brown Western>Brown Wellington>Southport>Brown Armitage
center, middle, aim, intention	noun	Racine>Blue Clinton>Racine
challenge, face-off	noun	Blue Grand>Logan Square
challenge, face, defy	verb	Blue Grand>Logan Square
change	noun	Green Oak Park>Green Clinton
change	verb	Green Oak Park>Green Clinton
city	noun	Francisco>Paulina

clay, mud, softness	noun	South Boulevard>Dempster
cloth	adj.	Blue Western>Blue Addison>Logan Square
clothe	verb	Blue Western>Blue Addison>Logan Square
clothing, cloth, fabric	noun	Blue Western>Blue Addison>Logan Square
cold	adj.	Orange Kedzie>Halsted
cold	noun	Orange Kedzie>Halsted
color, give depth/meaning	verb	Blue California>Blue Damen>Blue California
color, interest, intrigue, depth	noun	Blue California>Blue Damen>Blue California
colorful, interesting, intriguing, profound	adj	Blue California>Blue Damen>Blue California
contain	verb	Forest Park>Blue Clinton
content, item	noun	Forest Park>Blue Clinton

continue, endure	verb	Green Kedzie>51st
control	noun	Purple Chicago>Purple Diversey
control	verb	Purple Chicago>Purple Diversey
cook	verb	King Drive>Green Roosevelt
cool	verb	Orange Kedzie>Halsted
count	verb	Purple Armitage>Purple Wilson
cover, disguise, mask	noun	Logan Square>Blue Belmont>Logan Square
create, make	verb	Blue Belmont>Blue Chicago
created	adj.	Blue Belmont>Blue Chicago
creation	noun	Blue Belmont>Blue Chicago
cultural, societal	adj.	Logan Square>Division
culture, society	noun	Logan Square>Division
dangle, hang	verb	Blue Cicero>Blue Western
dibs	noun	Purple Diversey>Purple Howard>Purple Chicago

digest, process	verb	UIC-Halstead>Kedzie-Homan>UIC-Halstead
digestion, process	noun	UIC-Halstead>Kedzie-Homan>UIC-Halstead
disavow, shun, reject	verb	Brown Addison>Brown Belmont>Red Addison
do good	verb	18th>Polk
do, act	verb	Green Clinton>Green Morgan>Green Ashland>Green Clinton
drink	verb	Red Damen>Red Grand
drink	noun	Wilson>Sheridan
earthy	adj.	Dempster>Davis
east	noun	Harlem/Lake>Green Clinton
east, eastern	adj.	Harlem/Lake>Green Clinton
eat	verb	Red Grand>Red Damen
elongate	verb	Red Howard>47th

endurance	noun	Green Kedzie>51st
enlarge	verb	Cermak-Chinatown>95th/Dan Ryan
essential, necessary	adj.	54th/Cermak>Pink Clinton
examination, test, try	noun	Laramie>Green Kedzie
examine, test out, try out	verb	Laramie>Green Kedzie
exchange, trade, barter	verb	Purple Sedgwick>Purple Wellington>Purple Chicago
exchange, trade, barter	noun	Purple Sedgwick>Purple Wellington>Purple Chicago
flexibility	noun	Orange Western>35th/Archer
flexible	adj.	Orange Western>35th/Archer
food	noun	King Drive>Green Roosevelt
fresh	adj.	Central>Noyes
friend	noun	Central Park>Pink Damen

frog, toad, amphibian	noun	South Boulevard>Dempster>South Boulevard
front	noun	Red Addison>Red Fullerton>Brown Addison
front, fore	adj.	Red Addison>Red Fullerton>Brown Addison
fun, amusement	noun	Blue Damen>Logan Square
fun, amusing	adj.	Blue Damen>Logan Square
function, work	verb	Irving Park>Paulina
gastronomic	adj.	King Drive>Green Roosevelt
go	verb	Green Kedzie>Green Clinton
good	adj.	18th>Polk
good	noun	18th>Polk
grab	verb	Indiana>Orange Ashland
ground	noun	Red Grand>Red Chicago>Red Grand>Red Chicago

group together, unite, crowd	verb	North/Clybourn>Red Belmont>Red Fullerton
group, communal	adj.	North/Clybourn>Red Belmont>Red Fullerton
group, crowd	noun	North/Clybourn>Red Belmont>Red Fullerton
hair	noun	Blue Cicero>Blue Western
hand	noun	Illinois Medical District>Racine
hang, dangle	verb	North/Clybourn>Red Addison
happen, occur	verb	Cermak-Chinatown>Sox-35th
happy	adj.	Pink Cicero>Pink Western
have fun	verb	Blue Damen>Logan Square
head, leader, chief	noun	Sox-35th>Red Addison
health	noun	Illinois Medical District>UIC-Halsted>Illinois Medical Destrict
healthy	adj.	Illinois Medical District>UIC-Halsted>Illinois Medical Destrict

hear	verb	Racine>UIC-Halsted>Blue Western>Racine
heard	adj.	Racine>UIC-Halsted>Blue Western>Racine
heat	noun	Orange Roosevelt>Halsted>Orange Roosevelt
heat	verb	Orange Roosevelt>Halsted>Orange Roosevelt
height	noun	Red Chicago>Red Howard
heirloom, treasure, antiquity	noun	Oak Park>Harlem/Lake
hidden, covered, masked	adj.	Logan Square>Blue Belmont>Logan Square
hide, cover, mask	verb	Logan Square>Blue Belmont>Logan Square
high	adj.	Red Chicago>Red Howard

Term	Part of speech	Route
hill, bump, protuberance	noun	Red Grand>Thorndale
hold	verb	Illinois Medical District>Racine
hope	noun	Green Kedzie>Green Morgan>Green Ashland
hope	verb	Green Kedzie>Green Morgan>Green Ashland
hopeful	adj.	Green Kedzie>Green Morgan>Green Ashland
horse	noun	Roosevelt>Indiana>35th-Bronzeville-IIT Orange
hot	adj.	Roosevelt>Halsted>Orange Roosevelt
human, humane	adj.	Brown Chicago>Brown Diversey
humble	adj.	Brown Chicago>Brown Addison
humility	noun	Brown Chicago>Brown Addison
innovate	verb	79th>Red Garfield

inside	noun	Racine>Blue Clinton
inspire, liven up	verb	Ashland/63rd>35th-Bronzeville-IIT
instruct, explain	verb	Granville>Argyle
instruction, explanation	noun	Granville>Argyle
intend, concentrate, focus	verb	Loyola>Jarvis
intent, concentrated, focused	adj.	Loyola>Jarvis
intention, concentration, focus	noun	Loyola>Jarvis
intently	adv.	Loyola>Jarvis
keep, guard	verb	Merchandise Mart>Brown Chicago
kitty-corner	noun	Blue Grand>Logan Square
know	verb	Yellow Howard>Dempster-Skokie>Yellow Howard
knowledge	noun	Yellow Howard>Dempster-Skokie>Yellow Howard
land, soil, sediment	noun	Dempster>Davis
language, map	noun	Berwyn>Thorndale>Red Grand

lead, be at the head of	verb	Sox-35th>Red Addison
leaf, sheet, page	noun	Main>Central
left	adj.	Green Garfield>Ashland/63rd
left	noun	Green Garfield>Ashland/63rd
length	noun	Red Howard>47th
lie (down)	verb	Red Addison>North/Clybourn
like, enjoy, take pleasure in	verb	Kostner>Pink Western
like, interest, enjoyment, pleasure	noun	Kostner>Pink Western
local	adj.	Brown Armitage>Brown Chicago
long	adj.	Red Howard>47th
love	noun	Pink Ashland>Pink Morgan
love	verb	Pink Ashland>Pink Morgan
low	adj.	Red Chicago>Clark/Division
machine	noun	Irving Park>Paulina
made up, dressed up, dressed formally	adj.	Division>Blue Grand>Division>Blue Grand
main, principal, chief	adj.	Sox-35th>Red Addison

mammal	noun	Wilson>Lawrence>Wilson Brown
manipulate, use (a tool)	verb	Armitage>Diversey>Brown Armitage
manuscript, document	noun	87th>Red Garfield>87th
market, bazaar	noun	Merchandise Mart>Brown Sedgwick
meal	noun	Red Grand>Red Damen
measure	verb	Halsted>35th/Archer>Halsted
measurement	noun	Halsted>35th/Archer>Halsted
meet	verb	Pink Ashland>Pink Clinton>Green Ashland
meeting	noun	Pink Ashland>Pink Clinton>Green Ashland
mix (drinks)	verb	Wilson>Sheridan
monetary	adj.	Purple Sedgwick>Purple Armitage
money	noun	Purple Sedgwick>Purple Armitage

necessity	noun	54th/Cermak>Pink Clinton
negative, pessimistic	adj.	Red Wilson>Bryn Mawr
new	adj.	79th>Red Garfield
next to	noun	Green Clinton>Green Ashland
nice, lovely	adj.	Pink California>Pink Morgan
noise, sound	noun	Racine>UIC-Halsted>Blue Western>Racine
north	noun	95th/Dan Ryan>Red Howard
north, northern	adj.	95th/Dan Ryan>Red Howard
nothing	noun	Red Grand>Red Chicago
novelty	noun	79th>Red Garfield
number	noun	Purple Armitage>Purple Wilson
old	adj.	Oak Park>Harlem/Lake
orbit, maintain relevance	verb	Francisco>Brown Montrose
organ	noun	UIC-Halstead>Blue Western>UIC-Halstead
outside, outdoors	noun	Blue Clinton>Racine

76

parent	noun	Illinois Medical District>Blue Damen
parental	adj.	Illinois Medical District>Blue Damen
permit, allow	verb	Indiana>King Drive
permit, ticket	noun	Indiana>King Drive
person, human	noun	Brown Chicago>Brown Diversey
pessimism	noun	Red Wilson>Bryn Mawr
phenomenon, occurrence	noun	Cermak-Chinatown>Sox-35th
pigment, makeup	noun	Division>Blue Grand>Division>Blue Grand
pigment, put on makeup	verb	Division>Blue Grand>Division>Blue Grand
place, area, location	noun	Brown Armitage>Brown Chicago
protect	verb	Pink Damen>Pink Ashland
protection	noun	Pink Damen>Pink Ashland
protective	adj.	Pink Damen>Pink Ashland

purchase, acquisition, buy	noun	Purple Belmont>Purple Diversey
read	verb	Main>Central
		Clark/Division>Red
reflect	verb	Grand>Clark/Division>Red
		Grand
		Clark/Division>Red
reflection	noun	Grand>Clark/Division>Red
		Grand
refresh, freshen up	verb	Central>Noyes
relevance, orbit	noun	Francisco>Brown Montrose
relevant, orbital	adj.	Francisco>Brown Montrose
render obsolete	verb	Oak Park>Harlem/Lake
reptile	noun	South Boulevard>Main>South Boulevard
reptilian	adj.	South Boulevard>Main>South Boulevard
rest	noun	Kedzie-Homan>UIC-Halsted

rest, relax	verb	Kedzie-Homan>UIC-Halsted
ride, utter	verb	Ridgeland>Central
right (direction)	adj.	Green Garfield>Cottage Grove
right (direction)	noun	Green Garfield>Cottage Grove
rise	verb	Red Grand>Thorndale
rope, capture	noun	Brown Western>Brown Wellington>Southport>Brown Armitage
safe	adj.	Pink Ashland>Pink Clinton
safety	noun	Pink Ashland>Pink Clinton
same	adj.	Green Ashland>Green Clinton
see, have an opinion	verb	Ashland>Green California>Ashland>California
seen, subjective	adj.	Ashland>Green California>Ashland>California
shop	verb	Brown Sedgwick>Merchandise Mart>Brown Sedgwick

shrink, cut down	verb	Cermak-Chinatown>47th
sight, view, perspective, opinion	noun	Ashland>Green California>Ashland>California
size	noun	Cermak-Chinatown>95th/Dan Ryan
sleep	noun	Harlem2>Harlem1
sleep	verb	Harlem2>Harlem1
sleep, related to sleep, sleepy	adj.	Harlem2>Harlem1
sleepily	adv.	Harlem2>Harlem1
slide, ski	verb	Green Kedzie>Green Oak Park
small, few	adj.	Cermak-Chinatown>Red 47th
soft	adj.	South Boulevard>Dempster
soften	noun	South Boulevard>Dempster
south	noun	Red Howard>95th/Dan Ryan
south, southern	adj.	Red Howard>95th/Dan Ryan
speak, talk, say, interact with a geographical area	verb	Berwyn>Thorndale>Red Grand

spirit, soul	noun	Ashland/63rd>35th-Bronzeville-IIT
spiritual, inspired	adj.	Ashland/63rd>35th-Bronzeville-IIT
		Brown Belmont>Brown
station, node	noun	Fullerton>Brown
		Wellington>Brown Diversey
		Brown Sedgwick>Merchandise
store, boutique, shop	noun	Mart>Brown Sedgwick
		Red Addison>Red
support	noun	Fullerton>Brown Addison
		Red Addison>Red
support	verb	Fullerton>Brown Addison
		Red Addison>Red
supportive	adj.	Fullerton>Brown Addison
		Green Roosevelt>35th-Bronzeville-
thing, matter, affair	noun	IIT
think	verb	Yellow Howard>Dempster-Skokie
though	noun	Yellow Howard>Dempster-Skokie

throw	verb	Cermak-McCormick Place>Green 47th
tie, capture	verb	Brown Western>Brown Wellington>Southport>Brown Armitage
time	noun	Pink Pulaski>Pink Damen>54th/Cermak
tool	noun	Brown Armitage>Brown Diversey>Brown Armitage
travel	verb	Orange Roosevelt>Midway
travel, trip	noun	Orange Roosevelt>Midway
tried, attempted	adj.	Green Kedzie>Green Clinton>Green Kedzie
try, attempt	noun	Green Kedzie>Green Clinton>Green Kedzie
try, attempt	verb	Green Kedzie>Green Clinton>Green Kedzie

use, employ, utilize	verb	Brown Diversey>Southport
use, end, function	noun	Brown Diversey>Southport
wait	verb	Red Fullerton>Berwyn
wait, spell	noun	Red Fullerton>Berwyn
walk	verb	Orange Roosevelt>Halsted
walk, promenade	noun	Orange Roosevelt>Halsted
weigh	verb	Halsted>Orange Ashland>Halsted
weight	noun	Halsted>Orange Ashland>Halsted
west	noun	Green Clinton>Harlem/Lake
west, western	adj.	Green Clinton>Harlem/Lake
whack, bizarre, messed up, wrong (morally)	adj.	Green California>Green Cicero
wide	adj.	35th/Archer>Orange Western
width	noun	35th/Archer>Orange Western

yellow	adj.	Yellow Howard>Oakton-Skokie>Yellow Howard>Dempster-Skokie
yellow	noun	Yellow Howard>Oakton-Skokie>Yellow Howard>Dempster-Skokie

CTA-English

Cermak-Chinatown>Red Garfield	noun	ability
18th>Polk	verb	do good
18th>Polk	adj.	good
18th>Polk	noun	good
35th/Archer>Orange Western	adj.	wide
35th/Archer>Orange Western	noun	width
54th/Cermak>Pink Clinton	adj.	essential, necessary
54th/Cermak>Pink Clinton	noun	necessity
79th>Red Garfield	verb	innovate
79th>Red Garfield	adj.	new
79th>Red Garfield	noun	novelty
87th>Red Garfield>87th	noun	manuscript, document
95th/Dan Ryan>Red Howard	adj.	north, northern
95th/Dan Ryan>Red Howard	noun	north
Ashland/63rd>35th-Bronzeville-IIT	verb	inspire, liven up

Ashland/63rd>35th-Bronzeville-IIT	noun	spirit, soul
Ashland/63rd>35th-Bronzeville-IIT	adj.	spiritual, inspired
Ashland>Green California>Ashland>California	verb	see, have an opinion
Ashland>Green California>Ashland>California	adj.	seen, subjective
Ashland>Green California>Ashland>California	noun	sight, view, perspective, opinion
Berwyn>Thorndale>Red Grand	noun	language, map
Berwyn>Thorndale>Red Grand	verb	speak, talk, say, interact with a geographical area
Blue Belmont>Blue Chicago	verb	create, make
Blue Belmont>Blue Chicago	adj.	created
Blue Belmont>Blue Chicago	noun	creation
Blue California>Blue Damen>Blue California	noun	color, interest, intrigue, depth

Blue California>Blue Damen>Blue California	verb	color, give depth/meaning
Blue California>Blue Damen>Blue California	adj	colorful, interesting, intriguing, profound
Blue Chicago>Blue Western	noun	art
Blue Chicago>Blue Western	adj.	artistic
Blue Cicero>Blue Western	verb	dangle, hang
Blue Cicero>Blue Western	noun	hair
Blue Clinton>Racine	noun	outside, outdoors
Blue Clinton>UIC-Halsted	adj.	bodily, corporeal
Blue Clinton>UIC-Halsted	noun	body
Blue Damen>Logan Square	adj.	fun, amusing
Blue Damen>Logan Square	noun	fun, amusement
Blue Damen>Logan Square	verb	have fun
Blue Grand>Logan Square	noun	challenge, face-off
Blue Grand>Logan Square	verb	challenge, face, defy
Blue Grand>Logan Square	noun	kitty-corner

Blue Western>Blue Addison>Logan Square	adj.	cloth
Blue Western>Blue Addison>Logan Square	verb	clothe
Blue Western>Blue Addison>Logan Square	noun	clothing, cloth, fabric
Brown Addison>Brown Belmont>Red Addison	noun	behind, back, rear
Brown Addison>Brown Belmont>Red Addison	verb	disavow, shun, reject
Brown Armitage>Brown Chicago	adj.	local
Brown Armitage>Brown Chicago	noun	place, area, location
Brown Armitage>Brown Diversey>Brown Armitage	noun	tool
Brown Armitage>Diversey>Brown Armitage	verb	manipulate, use (a tool)

Brown Belmont>Brown Fullerton>Brown Wellington>Brown Diversey	noun	station, node
Brown Chicago>Brown Addison	adj.	humble
Brown Chicago>Brown Addison	noun	humility
Brown Chicago>Brown Diversey	adj.	human, humane
Brown Chicago>Brown Diversey	noun	person, human
Brown Chicago>Brown Kedzie	noun	building, structure, statue
Brown Chicago>Brown Kedzie	verb	build, construct
Brown Diversey>Southport	noun	use, end, function
Brown Diversey>Southport	verb	use, employ, utilize
Brown Sedgwick>Merchandise Mart>Brown Sedgwick	verb	shop
Brown Sedgwick>Merchandise Mart>Brown Sedgwick	noun	store, boutique, shop

Brown Western>Brown Wellington>Southport>Brown Armitage	adj.	captured, tamed
Brown Western>Brown Wellington>Southport>Brown Armitage	noun	rope, capture
Brown Western>Brown Wellington>Southport>Brown Armitage	verb	tie, capture
Central Park>Pink Damen	noun	friend
Central Park>Polk	adj.	beautiful, pretty
Central Park>Polk	noun	beauty, prettiness
Central>Noyes	noun	air, freshness
Central>Noyes	adj.	fresh
Central>Noyes	verb	refresh, freshen up
Cermak-Chinatown>47th	verb	shrink, cut down

Cermak-Chinatown>95th/Dan Ryan	adj.	big, large
Cermak-Chinatown>95th/Dan Ryan	verb	enlarge
Cermak-Chinatown>95th/Dan Ryan	noun	size
Cermak-Chinatown>Red 47th	adj.	small, few
Cermak-Chinatown>Red Garfield	adj.	able
Cermak-Chinatown>Red Garfield	verb	can
Cermak-Chinatown>Sox-35th	verb	happen, occur
Cermak-Chinatown>Sox-35th	noun	phenomenon, occurrence
Cermak-McCormick Place>Green 47th	verb	throw
Clark/Division>Red Grand>Clark/Division>Red Grand	noun	bean

Clark/Division>Red Grand>Clark/Division>Red Grand	verb	reflect
Clark/Division>Red Grand>Clark/Division>Red Grand	noun	reflection
Dempster-Skokie>Yellow Howard	noun	belief
Dempster-Skokie>Yellow Howard	verb	believe
Dempster>Davis	adj.	earthy
Dempster>Davis	noun	land, soil, sediment
Division>Blue Grand>Division>Blue Grand	adj.	made up, dressed up, dressed formally
Division>Blue Grand>Division>Blue Grand	noun	pigment, makeup
Division>Blue Grand>Division>Blue Grand	verb	pigment, put on makeup
Forest Park>Blue Clinton	noun	content, item

Forest Park>Blue Clinton	verb	contain
Francisco>Brown Montrose	verb	orbit, maintain relevance
Francisco>Brown Montrose	adj.	relevant, orbital
Francisco>Brown Montrose	noun	relevance, orbit
Francisco>Paulina	noun	city
Granville>Argyle	verb	instruct, explain
Granville>Argyle	noun	instruction, explanation
Green Ashland>Green Clinton	adj.	same
Green California>Green Ashland	noun	alcohol, alcoholic drink
Green California>Green Ashland	adj.	alcoholic
Green California>Green Ashland	verb	brew, ferment
Green California>Green Cicero	adj.	whack, bizarre, messed up, wrong (morally)
Green Clinton>Green Ashland	noun	next to
Green Clinton>Green Morgan>Green Ashland>Green Clinton	noun	act, action

Green Clinton>Green Morgan>Green Ashland>Green Clinton	adj.	active
Green Clinton>Green Morgan>Green Ashland>Green Clinton	adv.	actively
Green Clinton>Green Morgan>Green Ashland>Green Clinton	verb	do, act
Green Clinton>Harlem/Lake	adj.	west, western
Green Clinton>Harlem/Lake	noun	west
Green Garfield>Ashland/63rd	adj.	left
Green Garfield>Ashland/63rd	noun	left
Green Garfield>Cottage Grove	adj.	right (direction)
Green Garfield>Cottage Grove	noun	right (direction)
Green Kedzie>51st	noun	endurance
Green Kedzie>51st	verb	continue, endure

Green Kedzie>Green Clinton	verb	go
Green Kedzie>Green Clinton>Green Kedzie	adj.	tried, attempted
Green Kedzie>Green Clinton>Green Kedzie	noun	try, attempt
Green Kedzie>Green Clinton>Green Kedzie	verb	try, attempt
Green Kedzie>Green Morgan>Green Ashland	noun	hope
Green Kedzie>Green Morgan>Green Ashland	verb	hope
Green Kedzie>Green Morgan>Green Ashland	adj.	hopeful
Green Kedzie>Green Oak Park	verb	slide, ski
Green Oak Park>Green Clinton	noun	change
Green Oak Park>Green Clinton	verb	change

Green Roosevelt>35th-Bronzeville-IIT	noun	thing, matter, affair
Halsted>35th/Archer>Halsted	verb	measure
Halsted>35th/Archer>Halsted	noun	measurement
Halsted>Orange		
Ashland>Halsted	verb	weigh
Halsted>Orange		
Ashland>Halsted	noun	weight
Harlem/Lake>Green Clinton	adj.	east, eastern
Harlem/Lake>Green Clinton	noun	east
Harlem2>Harlem1	adj.	sleep, related to sleep, sleepy
Harlem2>Harlem1	noun	sleep
Harlem2>Harlem1	verb	sleep
Harlem2>Harlem1	adv.	sleepily
Illinois Medical District>Blue Damen	verb	beget, parent, father, mother

Illinois Medical District>Blue Damen	noun	parent
Illinois Medical District>Blue Damen	adj.	parental
Illinois Medical District>Racine	noun	hand
Illinois Medical District>Racine	verb	hold
Illinois Medical District>UIC-Halsted>Illinois Medical Destrict	noun	health
Illinois Medical District>UIC-Halsted>Illinois Medical Destrict	adj.	healthy
Indiana>King Drive	verb	permit, allow
Indiana>King Drive	noun	permit, ticket
Indiana>Orange Ashland	noun	between
Indiana>Orange Ashland	verb	grab
Irving Park>Paulina	verb	function, work
Irving Park>Paulina	noun	machine
Kedzie-Homan>UIC-Halsted	noun	rest

Kedzie-Homan>UIC-Halsted	verb	rest, relax
King Drive>Green Roosevelt	verb	cook
King Drive>Green Roosevelt	noun	food
King Drive>Green Roosevelt	adj.	gastronomic
Kostner>Pink Western	verb	like, enjoy, take pleasure in
Kostner>Pink Western	noun	like, interest, enjoyment, pleasure
Laramie>Green Kedzie	noun	examination, test, try
Laramie>Green Kedzie	verb	examine, test out, try out
Logan Square>Blue Belmont>Logan Square	noun	cover, disguise, mask
Logan Square>Blue Belmont>Logan Square	verb	hide, cover, mask
Logan Square>Blue Belmont>Logan Square	adj.	hidden, covered, masked
Logan Square>Division	adj.	cultural, societal
Logan Square>Division	noun	culture, society
Loyola>Jarvis	verb	intend, concentrate, focus

Loyola>Jarvis	adj.	intent, concentrated, focused
Loyola>Jarvis	noun	intention, concentration, focus
Loyola>Jarvis	adv.	intently
Main>Central	noun	leaf, sheet, page
Main>Central	verb	read
Merchandise Mart>Brown Chicago	verb	keep, guard
Merchandise Mart>Brown Sedgwick	noun	market, bazaar
North/Clybourn>Red Addison	noun	above, overhead
North/Clybourn>Red Addison	verb	hang, dangle
North/Clybourn>Red Belmont>Red Fullerton	adj.	group, communal
North/Clybourn>Red Belmont>Red Fullerton	noun	group, crowd
North/Clybourn>Red Belmont>Red Fullerton	verb	group together, unite, crowd

Noyes>Davis	noun	arm, branch
Oak Park>Harlem/Lake	noun	heirloom, treasure, antiquity
Oak Park>Harlem/Lake	adj.	old
Oak Park>Harlem/Lake	verb	render obsolete
Orange Kedzie>Halsted	adj.	cold
Orange Kedzie>Halsted	noun	cold
Orange Kedzie>Halsted	verb	cool
Orange Roosevelt>Halsted	noun	walk, promenade
Orange Roosevelt>Halsted	verb	walk
Orange Roosevelt>Halsted>Orange Roosevelt	noun	heat
Orange Roosevelt>Halsted>Orange Roosevelt	verb	heat

Orange Roosevelt>Halsted>Orange Roosevelt	adj.	hot
Orange Roosevelt>Midway	noun	travel, trip
Orange Roosevelt>Midway	verb	travel
Orange Western>35th/Archer	verb	bend
Orange Western>35th/Archer	noun	flexibility
Orange Western>35th/Archer	adj.	flexible
Pink Ashland>Pink Clinton	adj.	safe
Pink Ashland>Pink Clinton	noun	safety
Pink Ashland>Pink Clinton>Green Ashland	verb	meet
Pink Ashland>Pink Clinton>Green Ashland	noun	meeting
Pink Ashland>Pink Morgan	noun	love
Pink Ashland>Pink Morgan	verb	love
Pink California>Pink Morgan	adj.	nice, lovely

Pink Cicero>Pink Western	adj.	happy
Pink Damen>Pink Ashland	adj.	protective
Pink Damen>Pink Ashland	noun	protection
Pink Damen>Pink Ashland	verb	protect
Pink Pulaski>Pink Damen>54th/Cermak	noun	time
Purple Armitage>Purple Wilson	verb	count
Purple Armitage>Purple Wilson	noun	number
Purple Belmont>Purple Diversey	verb	buy
Purple Belmont>Purple Diversey	noun	purchase, acquisition, buy
Purple Chicago>Purple Diversey	noun	control
Purple Chicago>Purple Diversey	verb	control
Purple Chicago>Purple Wellington	adj.	business, business-related
Purple Chicago>Purple Wellington	noun	business

Purple Diversey>Purple Howard>Purple Chicago	verb	call dibs
Purple Diversey>Purple Howard>Purple Chicago	noun	dibs
Purple Sedgwick>Purple Armitage	adj.	monetary
Purple Sedgwick>Purple Armitage	noun	money
Purple Sedgwick>Purple Wellington>Purple Chicago	noun	exchange, trade, barter
Purple Sedgwick>Purple Wellington>Purple Chicago	verb	exchange, trade, barter
Racine>Blue Clinton	noun	inside
Racine>Blue Clinton>Racine	verb	aim (for), intend, mean
Racine>Blue Clinton>Racine	noun	center, middle, aim, intention
Racine>UIC-Halsted>Blue Western>Racine	verb	hear
Racine>UIC-Halsted>Blue Western>Racine	adj.	heard

Racine>UIC-Halsted>Blue Western>Racine	noun	noise, sound
Red Addison>North/Clybourn	noun	below, beneath
Red Addison>North/Clybourn	verb	lie (down)
Red Addison>Red Fullerton>Brown Addison	noun	front
Red Addison>Red Fullerton>Brown Addison	adj.	front, fore
Red Addison>Red Fullerton>Brown Addison	adj.	supportive
Red Addison>Red Fullerton>Brown Addison	noun	support
Red Addison>Red Fullerton>Brown Addison	verb	support
Red Chicago>Clark/Division	adj.	low
Red Chicago>North Clybourn	noun	all
Red Chicago>Red Howard	noun	height

Red Chicago>Red Howard	adj.	high
Red Damen>Red Grand	verb	drink
Red Fullerton>Berwyn	noun	wait, spell
Red Fullerton>Berwyn	verb	wait
Red Grand>Red Chicago	noun	nothing
Red Grand>Red Chicago>Red Grand>Red Chicago	verb	bury
Red Grand>Red Chicago>Red Grand>Red Chicago	noun	ground
Red Grand>Red Damen	verb	eat
Red Grand>Red Damen	noun	meal
Red Grand>Thorndale	adj.	bumpy
Red Grand>Thorndale	noun	hill, bump, protuberance
Red Grand>Thorndale	verb	rise
Red Howard>47th	noun	length
Red Howard>47th	adj.	long
Red Howard>47th	verb	elongate

Red Howard>95th/Dan Ryan	adj.	south, southern
Red Howard>95th/Dan Ryan	noun	south
Red Wilson>Bryn Mawr	adj.	negative, pessimistic
Red Wilson>Bryn Mawr	noun	pessimism
Ridgeland>Central	verb	ride, utter
Roosevelt>Indiana>35th-Bronzeville-IIT	noun	horse
South Boulevard>Dempster	noun	clay, mud, softness
South Boulevard>Dempster	adj.	soft
South Boulevard>Dempster	noun	soften
South Boulevard>Dempster>South Boulevard	adj.	amphibian
South Boulevard>Dempster>South Boulevard	noun	frog, toad, amphibian

South Boulevard>Main>South Boulevard	adj.	reptilian
South Boulevard>Main>South Boulevard	noun	reptile
Sox-35th>Red Addison	noun	head, leader, chief
Sox-35th>Red Addison	verb	lead, be at the head of
Sox-35th>Red Addison	adj.	main, principal, chief
UIC-Halstead>Blue Western>UIC-Halstead	noun	organ
UIC-Halstead>Kedzie-Homan>UIC-Halstead	noun	digestion, process
UIC-Halstead>Kedzie-Homan>UIC-Halstead	verb	digest, process
Wilson>Lawrence>Wilson	noun	mammal
Wilson>Sheridan	noun	drink
Wilson>Sheridan	verb	mix (drinks)
Yellow Howard>Dempster-Skokie	verb	think

Yellow Howard>Dempster-Skokie	noun	though
Yellow Howard>Dempster-Skokie>Yellow Howard	noun	knowledge
Yellow Howard>Dempster-Skokie>Yellow Howard	verb	know
Yellow Howard>Oakton-Skokie>Yellow Howard>Dempster-Skokie	adj.	yellow
Yellow Howard>Oakton-Skokie>Yellow Howard>Dempster-Skokie	noun	yellow

Phrasebook

"Meet me at the Bean"

*TI ...TF..G*Pink Ashland→Pink Clinton→Green
Ashland*EC...T*NFR....*S*Any1*H2F..EC...T*RNR...*GE*Clark/Divisi
on→Red Grand→Clark/Division→Red Grand*E2L...TO*

Go through the turnstile at Ashland (Pink Line). Board
the train and go from Ashland to Clinton (Pink Line), then switch
to the Green Line. Ride until Ashland (Green Line). As you ride,
tap your feet continuously and grab onto a handle or pole—ride
with your eyes closed. When you've gotten off at Ashland (Green
Line), get onto any train and ride for precisely one stop, again
while keeping your eyes closed. This time, you will hold one of
your palms to your face as you ride and sit for the duration.
Transfer to Clark/Division while keeping at least one hand in
your pocket. There, board a southbound train and go to Grand
(Red Line) while grabbing your ear and keeping your eyes
oriented to your left. When you've arrived at Grand (Red Line),
switch to a northbound train and return to Clark/Division. Don't
stop looking left. Don't stop grabbing your ear. You've gotten to
Clark/Division? Good, repeat. Go southbound again to Grand
and come back, all the while holding your ear and looking left.
When you've returned to Clark/Division a second time, go out
of the turnstile.

meet........Pink Ashland→Pink Clinton→Green Ashland

bean........Clark/Division→Red Grand→Clark/Division→
          Red Grand

I..............sit

pronoun isolator.....hand (palm) to face

you/y'all...grab handle, pole, etc.

The **imperative** is indicated by the speaker closing, and keeping closed, their eyes. (*EC*)

When the eyes of a speaker are closed for the duration or vast majority of a ride, the noun is interpreted as being in the **accusative**, the object of a sentence. (*EC*)

Eyes looking left indicates that the noun is in the **locative** case, indicating that the noun is the location of an event or another noun. (*E2L*)

When a speaker desires to isolate a pronoun, either to emphasize a pronoun or else to put one in a noun case besides that of the nominative, they must ride from one CTA stop to the next over (direction does not matter) and exit the train. At the same time, they must place an open hand to the face, with the tips of their fingers typically touching the cheek (*H2F*) and the back of the hand facing up or toward the speaker's face. Proper eye movements are used to indicate grammatical case.

Tapping one's feet indicates that the root ride is a verb.

Grabbing one's ear indicates that the ride is a noun.

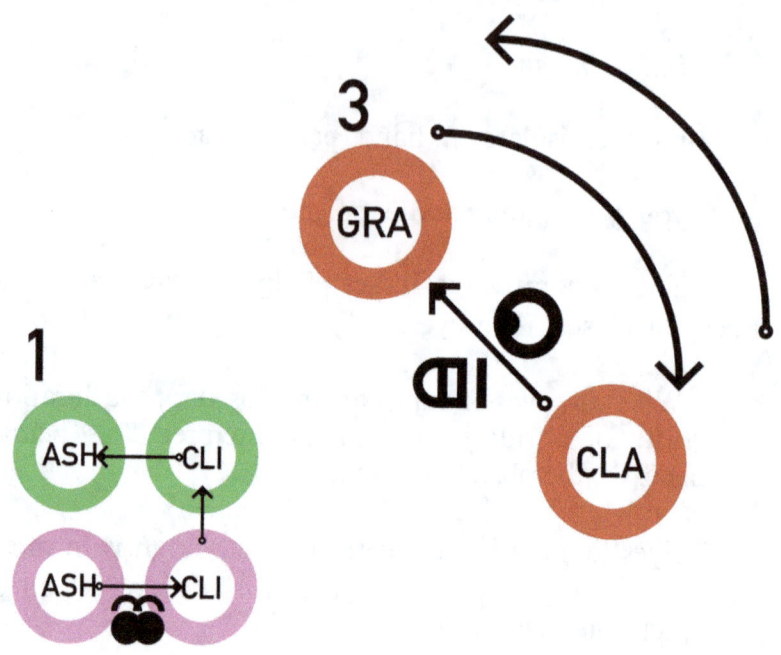

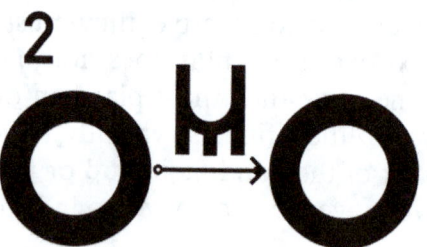

"I hope you'll have fun."

*TI...TF..S*Green Kedzie→Green Morgan→Green
Ashland...TNFR...Washington→Blue
Jackson...TNFR...*TF..G*Blue Damen→Logan Square...*TO*

Enter through the turnstile at Kedzie (Green Line). Ride to Morgan. Then go to Ashland. Do so as you tap your feet continuously. Do not stop. Once arrived at Ashland (Green Line), transfer to Washington. Ride to Jackson (Blue Line). There, transfer to Damen (Blue Line). Ride to Logan Square. Tap your feet continuously as you do so and grab onto a handle or pole. When you arrive, exit through the turnstile. Have fun.

hope: Green Kedzie→Green Morgan→Green Ashland

fun, have fun: Blue Damen→Logan Square

That (relative clause builder): Washington→Blue Jackson

I...............sit

you/y'all...grab handle, pole, etc.

When the eyes of a speaker are closed for the duration or vast majority of a ride, the noun is interpreted as being in the **accusative**, the object of a sentence. (*EC*)

Tapping one's feet indicates that the root ride is a verb.

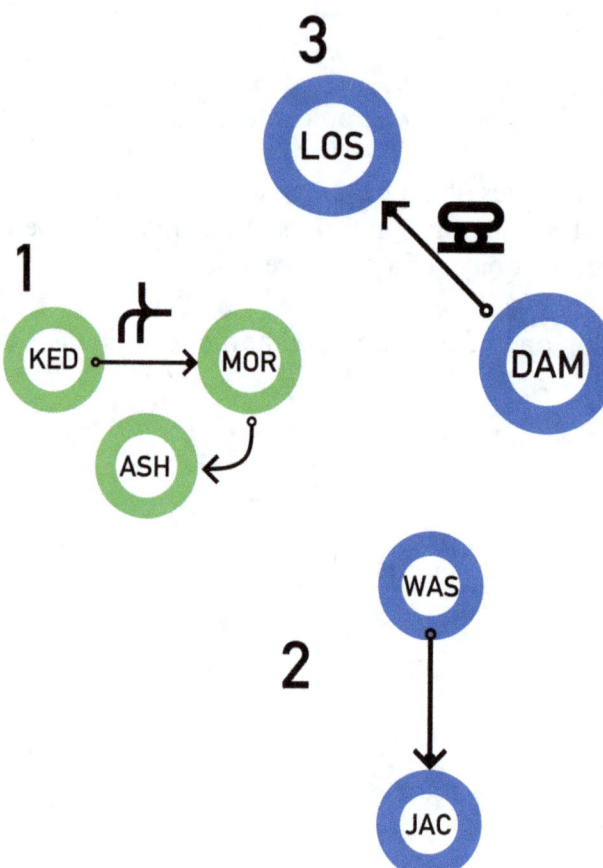

"Farewell, my love."

*TI...S*Any1*H2F..E2R...*TNFR...*GE*Pink Ashland→Pink Morgan...TNFR...*GE*Brown Chicago→Brown Diversey...*AH2F...TO*

At any station, go through the turnstile. Ride precisely one stop while holding the palm of your hand to your cheek. Keep your eyes turned to the right. Transfer to Ashland (Pink Line) and ride to Morgan while grabbing your ear. Get off there and transfer to Chicago (Brown Line). Ride to Diversey (Brown Line) while, again, grabbing your ear continuously. There, place your palm at a few inches' distance from your interlocutor's cheek, but never touch. If you're by yourself, mime. Exit through the turnstile. Farewell.

love.........Pink Ashland→Pink Morgan

person.....Brown Chicago→Brown Diversey

I...............sit

you/y'all...grab handle, pole, etc.

E2R..........genitive (possessive)

pronoun
isolator.....hand (palm) to face

Grabbing onto a handle or pole in the train indicates that the subject is 2nd person (you, y'all).

Tapping one's feet indicates that the root ride is a verb.

Grabbing one's ear indicates that the ride is a noun.

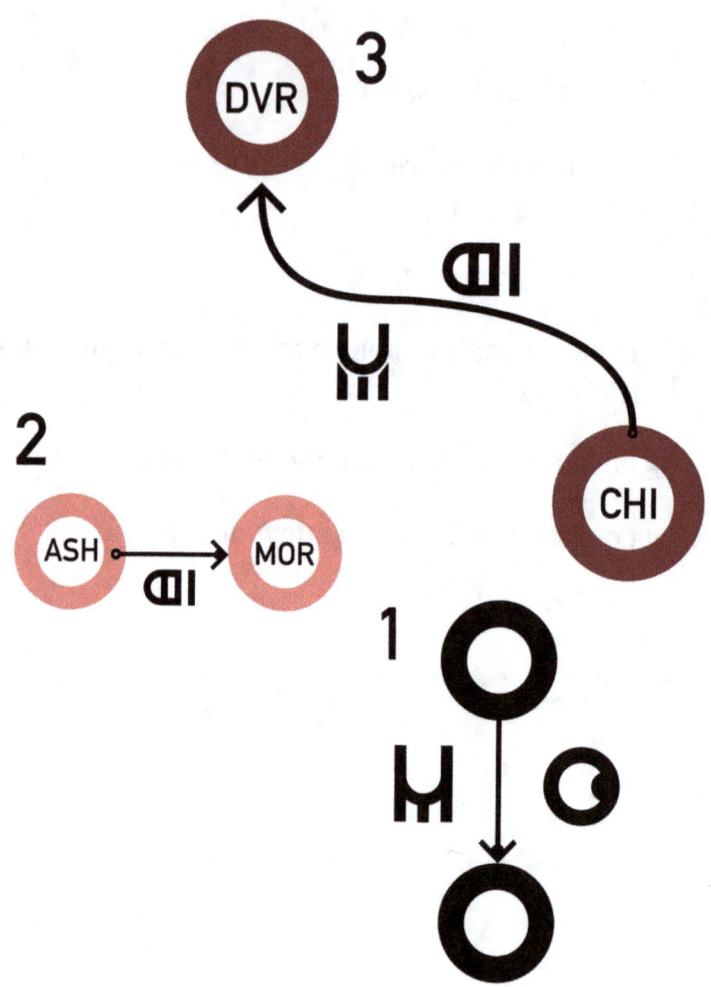

"Where can we buy tickets?"

TI... Lake→Red
Jackson...TNFR...Adams/Wabash→State/Lake*CntCW*
...TNFR... *GE*..Indiana→King Drive*EC*...TNFR....*S*Cermak-
Chinatown→Red Garfield*EO*... TNFR...*TF*..Green
Kedzie→Green Oak Park...*TO*

Walk through the turnstile at Lake. Take the train heading south to Jackson (Red Line). From there transfer to Adams/Wabash and ride the Loop counterclockwise to State/Lake. Head to Indiana and from there ride to King Drive while keeping your eyes closed. Make sure to hold onto your ear (it doesn't matter which one) as you complete this ride. When you get to King Drive, you can open your eyes and make another transfer to Cermak-Chinatown. When you get on the train, sit down and ride to Garfield (Red Line) while keeping your eyes open—forcefully and with intent. Transfer a final time to Kedzie (Green Line) and from there ride to Oak Park (Green Line). Get off and head out the exit.

where....Lake→Red Jackson

we..........sit

some.....Adams/Wabash→State/Lake CntCW

can........Cermak-Chinatown→Red Garfield

buy........Purple Belmont→Purple Diversey

ticket.....Indiana→King Drive

Grabbing onto a handle or pole in the train indicates that the subject is 2nd person (you, y'all).

Tapping one's feet indicates that the root ride is a verb.

Grabbing one's ear indicates that the ride is a noun.

Keeping one's eyes closed indicates that a noun is in the accusative case.

Keeping one's eyes open demonstrates that a verb is indicative.

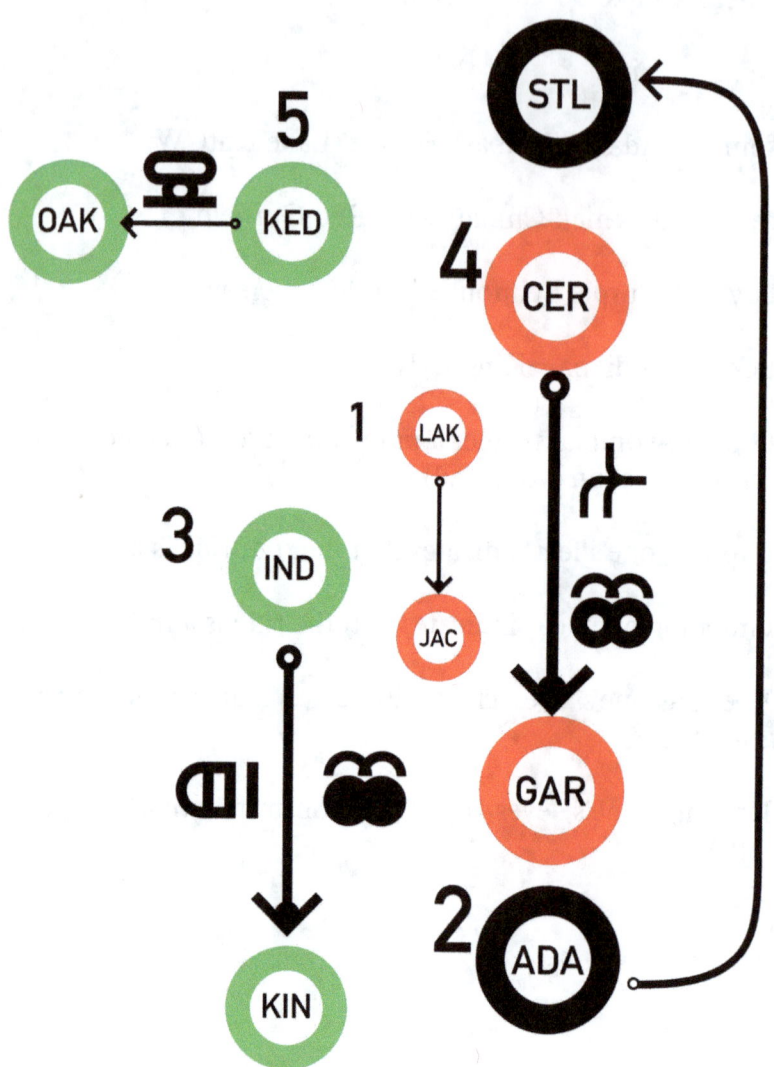

"Where is the library?"

TI ...TFOS.. 79th→Red Garfield→87th...TNFR...*GE..* Brown Chicago→Brown Kedzie*EO*...TNFR...Red Lake→Red Jackson... *TO*

Enter the 79th Street station and get on a train headed north. When you get on, tap a fist against its opposite shoulder. Ride all the way to Garfield (Red Line), get off and go south again, this time to the 87th Street station. Don't stop tapping that fist to the opposite shoulder. When you arrive at 87th, get off and stop tapping your fist to its opposite shoulder. Head over to Brown Chicago now. There, board a train and head to Brown Kedzie. When you board, grab an ear, whichever, and keep your eyes open. When you get there, you're going to need to head over to Lake (Red Line) and ride it south toward Jackson (Red Line). Get off the train there and head out of the station.

manuscript, document....69th→Red Garfield→87th

building, structure, statue, house..........Brown Chicago→Brown Kedzie

where.....Red Lake→Red Jackson

Grabbing one's ear indicates that the ride is a noun.

Keeping one's eyes open indicates that a noun is in the nominative case.

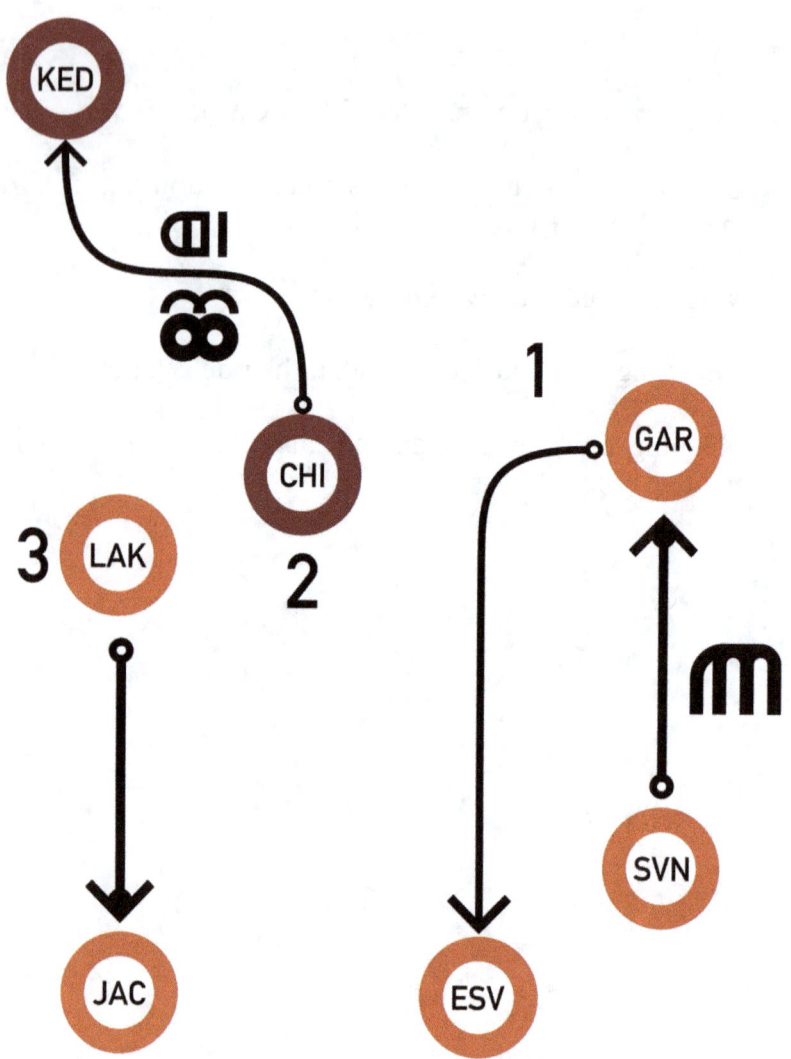

"What do you like to do?"

*TI...TF..G*Kostner→Pink Western*EO*...TNFR...*TF*..Green Clinton→Green Morgan→Green Ashland→Green Clinton*H2F*...TNFR...Washington→Blue Jackson*EC...TO*

Go ahead and go through the turnstile at Kostner. Board a train going east, toward the lake. Once on the train, grab onto to a pole or something and tap your feet as you ride along. Make sure to keep your eyes open, but not too much. Get off at Western (Pink Line) and then transfer over to Clinton (Green Line). Once you get to Clinton, board a train going west. Tap your feet on that train too, but this time don't grab onto anything. Instead, gently and continuously touch the tips of your fingers to your face. Get off at Morgan and then get back on to continue on to Ashland. Don't stop holding your hand to your face! Don't stop tapping those feet! Get off at Ashland and walk over the bridge to the other side of the tracks. Go back east to Clinton. You can stop tapping your feet and holding your fingers to your cheek while/if you're waiting on your next train but make sure to start again when you've got on the train going eastbound. Once you've gotten to Clinton, disembark. Head over to Washington head to Jackson while keeping your eyes closed. At Jackson, get off and exit the station.

like, enjoy, take pleasure in....Kostner→Pink Western

act, do..........Green Clinton→Green Morgan→Green Ashland→Green Clinton

what.....Washington→Blue Jackson

you/y'all...grab handle, pole, etc.

Tapping one's feet indicates that the root ride is a verb.

Keeping one's eyes open demonstrates that a verb is indicative.

When the eyes of a speaker are closed for the duration or vast majority of a ride, the noun is interpreted as being in the **accusative**, the object of a sentence. (*EC*)

Gently touching one's hand to one's face renders the verb is being treated as an infinitive or that it is being nominalized.

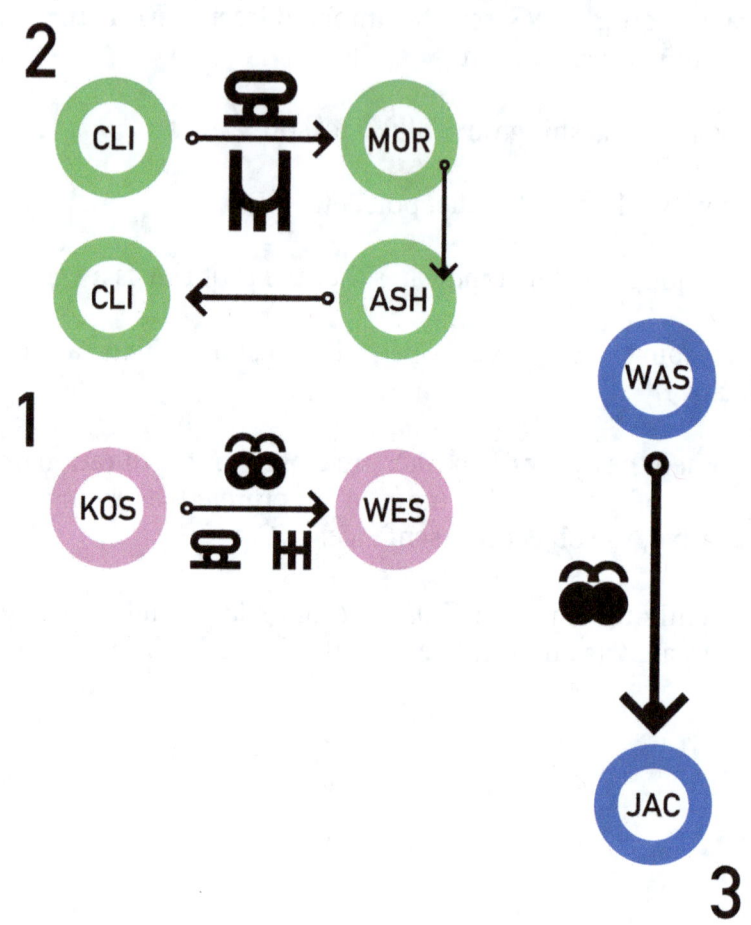

"Let's exchange phone numbers."

TI... *TF*..*S*Purple Sedgwick→Purple Wellington→Purple Chicago*EC*...TNFR...*TFOS*..Berwyn→Thorndale→Red Grand...TNFR...*GE*..Brown Armitage→Brown Diversey→Brown Armitage*E2R*...TNFR...*GE*..Purple Armitage→Purple Wilson*EC*...*TO*

Please enter Sedgwick (Purple Line). You're going to need to ride from there to Wellington (Purple Line), then from Wellington to Chicago (Purple Line). Plan the time you'll be saying this sentence well, because this part of the Purple Line only operates during certain hours of the day. As you're riding between these three stations, find a seat, any seat, and make sure to keep your eyes closed for the duration of the ride. When you get to Chicago (Purple Line), somehow get to Berwyn, on the Red Line. Wait for the train going north. As you get on, place your fist to the opposite shoulder and just sort of tap it laxly. As you continue to tap your fist to its opposite shoulder, get off at Thorndale and ride south again to Grand (Red Line). There get off. Yes, you may stop tapping your fist to its opposite shoulder. Again, find some way to get to Armitage (Brown Line). Go to Diversey (Brown Line). At Diversey, change trains and go back to Armitage. You'll feel like you're playing pong. Do all of this while grabbing one of your ears and keeping your eyes turned to the right. Transfer to the Purple Line. From Armitage (Purple Line), go to Wilson (Purple Line). Again, grab onto one of your ears, but don't keep your eyes turned to the right. Keep them closed. You can get off the train at Wilson and exit out the turnstile. Good job.

exchange, trade, barter....Purple Sedgwick→Purple
                                    Wellington→Purple Chicago

linguistic, meant for speaking..........Berwyn→Thorndale→Red
                                    Grand

tool.....Brown Armitage→Brown Diversey→Brown Armitage

number.....Purple Armitage→Purple Wilson

we..........sit

Tapping one's feet indicates that the root ride is a verb.

Tapping one's fist against the opposite shoulder indicates that a root is being used adjectively.

The **imperative** is indicated by the speaker closing, and keeping closed, their eyes. (*EC*)

Grabbing one's ear indicates that the ride is a noun.

Keeping one's eyes fixed to the right (from the perspective of the viewer) means that the noun is being used in the genitive.

When the eyes of a speaker are closed for the duration or vast majority of a ride, the noun is interpreted as being in the **accusative**, the object of a sentence. (*EC*)

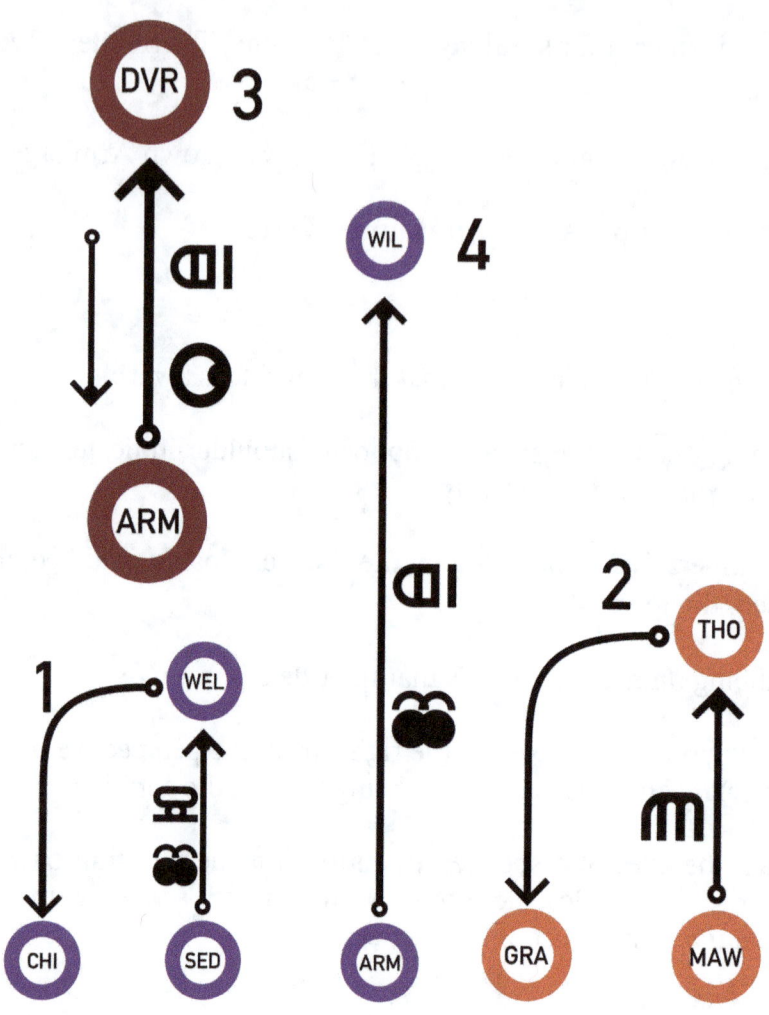

"Explain dibs to me, please."

TI ... TF..Granville→Argyle*EC*...TNFR...*GE*..Purple
Diversey→Purple Howard→Purple
Chicago*EC*...TNFR....*S*Any1*H2F*..*EWO*...PRAY...*TO*

Tap your card and go through the turnstile at Granville. Ride south toward Argyle. Do so while keeping your eyes closed. Also, tap your feet! Then, get over to Diversey (Purple Line) via any route you wish to take. Get on a train and go to Howard (Purple Line). At Howard, change trains again and go to Chicago. As you're riding these various trains, you must grab onto one of your ears and keep your eyes closed. Next, you will ride from any station you wish down precisely one stop. Sit down in the train your riding, while simultaneously keeping the tips of your fingers gently pressed up against your cheek. Your eyes must also be held wide open. It's okay if you look a bit deranged! When you get to the next station, get off and put your hands together as if you were praying. You've made your request. Now head out of the station.

instruct, explain....Granville→Argyle

dibs...........Purple Diversey→Purple Howard→Purple Chicago

Tapping one's feet indicates that the root ride is a verb.

Grabbing one's ear indicates that the ride is a noun.

Keeping one's eyes closed indicates that a noun is in the accusative case.

Keeping one's eyes wide open puts a noun in the **dative** case (makes it the indirect object of a phrase)

Placing one's hands in a prayer position, indicates that a polite request is being made.

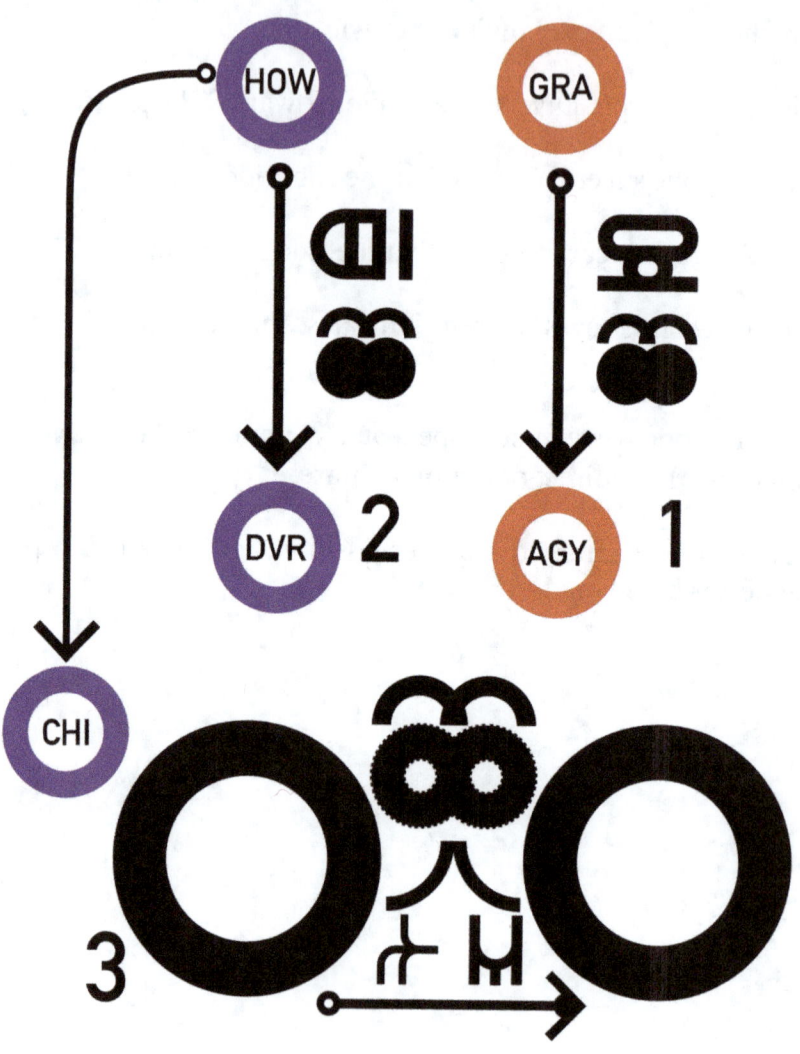

"How do I get to City Hall?"

*TI ... TF..S*Green Kedzie→Green
Clinton*EO...*TNFR...*TFOS..*Francisco→Paulina...TNFR...*TFO
S..*Sox-35th→Red Addison...TNFR...*GE..*Brown
Chicago→Brown Kedzie*LEC...*TNFR...LaSalle/Van
Buren→Quincy*CW...TO*

Kedzie (on the Green Line) is a really beautiful station. From there you can see the whole skyline. Try being there at either sunrise or sunset. The glimmer off the skyscrapers is quite breathtaking. Once you've had a nice look at the skyline, feel free to get on an eastbound train. When you get on the train take a seat and keep your eyes open. When you get there change lines. Change trains. Get to the Brown Line somehow. Board a train at Francisco. As you start this ride, start tapping your fist on the opposite shoulder. Ride to Paulina. Change trains. However, you like, get to Sox-35th. Embark on the next leg of your journey and, once more, tap your fist to your shoulder (continuously). Ride north. Get off at Addison (Red Line). Change trains again. Get to Chicago on the Brown Line. Get on a train going north. As you ride, grab onto your ear. Keep your left eye closed for the duration of the ride. Just your left eye, though. Transfer to another line just one last time. Get on to a train at LaSalle/Van Buren downtown. Ride to Quincy, using either Pink or Orange Lines. Get off at Quincy. Don't worry, you're not too far from City Hall.

go....Green Kedzie→Green Clinton

city..........Francisco→Paulina

main, principal, chief.....Sox-35th→Red Addison

building, structure, statue.....Brown Chicago→Brown Kedzie

how....LaSalle/Van Buren→Quincy

I..............sit

Tapping one's feet indicates that the root ride is a verb.

Keeping one's eyes open demonstrates that a verb is indicative.

Tapping one's fist against the opposite shoulder indicates that a root is being used as an adjective.

Grabbing one's ear indicates that the ride is a noun.

One keeps only the left eye closed in order to indicate that the noun is in the **allative** case (an action is happening in the direction of the noun in question.)

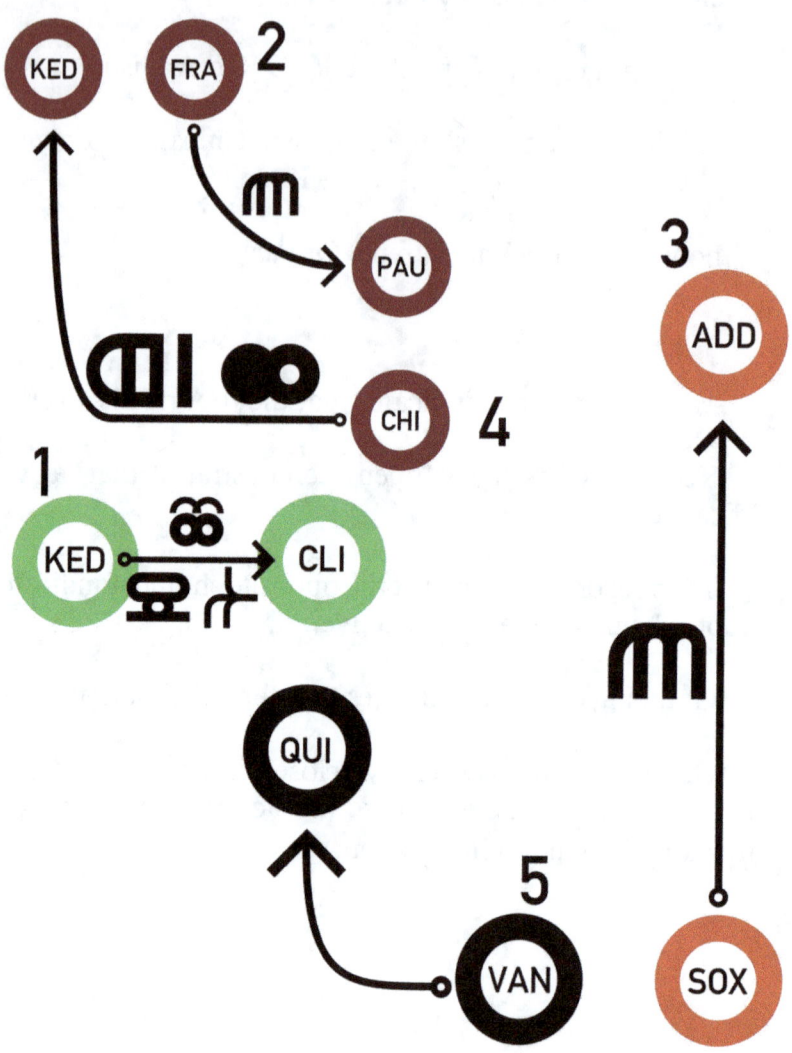

"Two tickets, please."

TI...*TFOS*..Ridgeland→Central...TNFR....*H2T2*..Indiana→
King Drive*EC*...PRAY...*TO*

      Scan your U-Pass or Ventra Card at Ridgeland. Take a train to Central. Then, go to Indiana. Get on a southbound train. In it, you will grab onto your ear while simultaneously tapping your hand on your thigh exactly twice. You may repeat this action if you wish, but ensure that each, individual action is separated out by an appropriate amount of time. As you speed along, close your eyes and keep them closed. Get off at King Drive. Once you're off, clap your hands together as if you're praying. Exit.

ride, for riding, for speaking....Ridgeland→Central

permit, ticket..........Indiana→King Drive

Tapping one's fist against the opposite shoulder indicates that a root is being used adjectively.

When specifying the number of a specific noun, the speaker places their hand to their thigh (*H2T*) instead of grabbing their ear (*GE*). They then tap your hand against your thigh for the appropriate number of times. In this instance, the number of taps is two, indicating that there are two of the specified noun.

When the eyes of a speaker are closed for the duration or vast majority of a ride, the noun is interpreted as being in the **accusative**, the object of a sentence. (*EC*)

Placing one's hands in a prayer position, indicates that a polite request is being made.

1

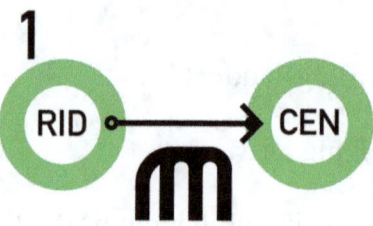

2

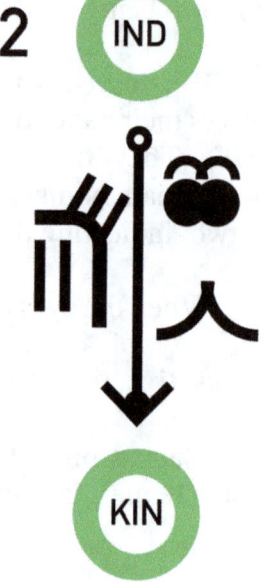